C000200834

CLIFFHANGER

THE LIFE AND TIMES OF JET HARRIS

Written by

MIKE COOK

**Grosvenor House
Publishing Limited**

This book is published by
Grosvenor House Publishing Ltd
Link House
140 The Broadway, Tolworth, Surrey, Kt6 7Ht.
www.grosvenorhousepublishing.co.uk

A CIP record for this book
is available from the British Library

ISBN 978-1-78623-915-0

For Ben, Sam, Craig

and

Wendy

Preface

Jet Harris was a member of probably the most successful instrumental band of all time -The Shadows. The good, bad and sad days, are all here. The affair that Cliff Richard had with his wife, Carol, which led to his lifelong fight against alcoholism and inevitably his fall from grace, Affectionately known as 'The Godfather' of the Electric Bass Guitar, he enjoyed both the fame and noteriety that went with the job, finally finding an inner peace in his later years on the Isle of Wight. A musical legend...

Introduction

"HOW NICE TO MEET YOU MR. HARRIS"

Ian 'Sammy' Samwell had just left Cliff's band to concentrate on song writing, and to continue with their management. A few months earlier he had been travelling from his mothers home in London Colney to Cliff's home in Cheshunt, sitting on the top deck of a Green Line Bus.

Like many young men of that time, he had been influenced by the music of Chuck Berry. His head was awash with the music of the day. His guitar lay beside him. Ian began to scribble down a few lyrics that were to become synonymous with the British rock scene for all time. By the time he reached Cliff's house the song was complete. It didn't take that long to write it only had one verse.

The song was MOVE IT... The rest is history.

Jet was touring with another name in the business Mickey Most and like the rest of the travelling players he watched with interest as the song began to climb up the charts. The tour lasted three weeks. The song began to climb higher and higher and eventually reached number two. It was September the year 1958.

Jet was somewhat young and impressionable, and had no idea of the fame and fortune tinged with heartache that was to come his way. The money may have gone but the memories have always remained. Jet always said where money was concerned it was easy come easy go. It just wasn't an object.

Jet's life was to revolve around the bottle for some forty years. Things could and should have been better, could and should have been different, but life is only what you make it. You only get out what you are prepared to put in. For Terry Harris time has moved on since those heady days. The whole world has stepped up a gear, everybody gasping for other people's air, with not nearly enough to go around.

Friends have come and gone, discarded like old broken toys. For forty years Jet's friends were been in bars. Any bar, it didn't really matter, they were always there to greet him. Having grown older and a lot wiser has mellowed the way he now looked at life. He knows that the scars will never really heal. Time though is a great healer.

We are constantly told that we are only passing through this earth plain getting ready for the next. Jet had confounded many people. He was there alive and kicking and above all still smiling.

Terence Harris was just an ordinary guy who just happened to be in the right place at the right time. It's as simple as that. Who knows where he might have been if that dark haired young man hadn't have asked him to join his band. Cliff saying,

'How nice to meet you Mr. Harris, would you consider coming to work for me?'

Diamonds are supposed to be forever. For most people they are. For good or for bad Jet has enjoyed his life. Being famous has opened up so many doors,

Let's open a few more....

HE FLIES LIKE A JET...........

July 6th 1939 was just like any other summers day. The war was just around the corner. The rumblings had been in the air for some time. Winnie and Bill Harris had both known hard times, and like so many families before them, had struggled to keep it together after the end of the Great War. Bill had been too young to be called up for the war effort and now sat like everyone else listening to the wireless with baited breath. Bill had never believed in violence and could never understand why people had to kill.

During the twenties, times were very hard. Everyday seemed an uphill struggle. Everyone tried hard to make ends meet. Britain had been renown for its tenacity and "bulldog spirit" and took the task of rebuilding with unflinching energy. People believed that better days weren't too far away. Times were really tough and no one really knew of the horrors and atrocities that were to befall our nation for a second time. The depression had seemed endless, and yet people always seemed to manage. There was always someone there to lend you a helping hand.

Wars were one thing. Winnie and Bill had something else on their mind. Terence Harris was about to make his first entrance. Honeypot Lane Hospital, Kingsbury was to be the birthplace for the only son of Winifred and William Harris.

Winnie had decided to name him Terence after her maiden name, and according to his father wanted to continue the family name. Winnie had in fact toyed with the idea of including the name McCloud another old Scottish name that seemed to pop up in their family tree. Winnie had visions of christening Terry with that name or at least hyphenating it with Harris.

McCloud-Harris what a handle that would have been. Bill had other ideas. and Harris it was. Come to think of it Jet McCloud Harris sounds a bit like an American country singer.

Terry's arrival caused the usual stir and the general rounds of uncles and aunties who would hug pat and generally maul the newborn infant. Terry's birth was quite normal and the extra mouth especially at such a critical time didn't seem to bother Winnie and Bill. To all intents and purposes life went on as normal.

The family home was No. 40 Brenthurst Road, Willesdon, a two storied building which Bill and Winnie rented at first, and later purchased for the princely sum of £425! Bill worked as a press tool setter for Dairy Supplies in Parkwood, making billycans and shell cases. Winnie was a typesetter with Harold Wesley Stationery Mill in Park Royal. Bill loved his job and used to bring home around £2.17 shillings (£2.85) a week. It was a skilled position, his working day beginning at seven in the morning, sometimes not returning until late at night. Bill would work any overtime he could, and the extra money always came in handy. Winnie on the other hand earned only 12/6d (62.5p).

To this day Terry wondered how they used to manage on such a low income, after all, that wouldn't have bought him three pints of beer!

It looked like war and coupled with that misfortune Winnie and Bill had to cope with a young Harris who's health was to take a turn for the worst. Terry's first year wasn't exactly what the doctor had ordered. At nine months old he was to return to hospital. Winnie and Bill had become a little concerned with his condition, which unbeknown to them was pretty serious at that time. The local hospital in Dog Lane was contacted and Terry was duly rushed in and placed immediately in an isolation ward. He had suspected diphtheria.

Survival was the name of the game and survive he did. He was to stay in isolation for some three months with Winnie and Bill visiting him regularly. Terry's condition being as it was meant that handling him was out of the question for fear of being infected themselves.

The anguish that they both endured during that period must have been quite unbearable. For the most part they could only sit and watch. Being an only child didn't help and Terry's frame being so small and fragile meant that he spent most of his time in an incubator.

The threat of war now upon them and Terry's condition was still somewhat precarious. Winnie and Bill had something else to contend with. For good measure Terry received a dose of dysentery! Being so small and extremely thin it was touch and go. To the relief of the medical team and more to the relief of his parents Terry was allowed home.

It was the day of the first mock air raids over London. The German invasion had been expected for some time now, and everybody was preparing for the worst. Winnie had doubts as to whether Terry would recognise anybody on his release from hospital, but her fears were allayed when he threw his arms out to her.

The skies over London were about to light up. The bombing seemed endless. It was incessant. Day after day, night after night. But life had to go on.

Winnie happened to be out one day pushing Terry along the road in a pram. Terry recalls that they were going to his grandmother's house in Kensington. Suddenly the sky opened up and all hell let loose. There were bombs going off everywhere. Winnie recalled that Terry's auntie Christine who was with them at the time was offered shelter in a nearby council house until the raid had finished.

The devastation was awful. Even at such a tender age Terry could still remember the smoke coming from the numerous buildings that were on fire. There didn't seem that a day went by without the sound of the fire engines racing across the smouldering city.

Being an only child had its advantages and of course, its disadvantages. However long and dark those days were to become, Terry always felt the safety and the security of the family home. To Terry it appeared as if the bombs were falling everywhere except on them.

No matter what, the food always seemed to be on the table. They as a family, although not rich never seemed to want for anything. When time allowed, Winnie and Bill continued to work, although most of Winnie's time was taken up looking after Terry. They were determined to carry on life as normal as possible.

Family visits continued whenever possible. Terry was still receiving his regular dosage of molly-coddling which was to continue for the first five years of his life.

He was protected from everything and everyone. He was well aware of the carnage around him, but he recalls that to him it was just a blur.

The night the first doodlebug hurtled over London was just like bonfire night. The whole sky was aglow. London wasn't the place to be. The air raids seemed endless. Winnie, Bill and Terry would spend most of their nights huddled beneath the stairs like most families at that time. As it seemed the safest place to be.

Their road too had its fair share of near misses. A land mine dropped onto the nearby technical college just around the corner. The explosion rattled the entire row of houses...but they managed to keep their windows!

Terry who by now was well aware of the surroundings recalled that next morning it literally looked like a bomb had hit it. Winnie and Bill were a little reluctant to let him out, although most lads even at that young age, somehow knew how to fend for themselves. The kids never seemed to be fully aware of the dangers that could have been lurking just around the corner. Too many nights were spent beneath those stairs with Winnie and Bill who never really seemed to show any signs of fear. They were of course as scared as the next family. they survived.

As a child Terry had to be pacified. Was it an omen? Who knows as Winnie used to feed him gripe water by the bottle, totally unaware that it contained some 97% alcohol!

Terry didn't disappoint he duly obliged and drank it as ordered; after all he wasn't old enough to argue!

Terry had managed to stay out of hospital for some time. That was about to change. He had by now reached the age of four and within the blink on an eye he was suddenly rushed to St. Mary's hospital with suspected tuberculosis.

Was this another omen?
A 'Shadow' had been discovered on his lung.

For the next year Terry was to find himself travelling with Bill or Winnie once a week for treatment. Terry was forced to drink two pints of malt a week. It was awful, but if he wanted to get better he had to drink it. Terry stuck to it rigidly. It took a long time, but with the due care and loving attention that he received he made a full recovery.

By now he had attained school age. Like most kids of the day, young Harris had to pick his way through the bombed streets climbing over rubble and rubbish to get to school. As kids they would always make their own fun. There was shrapnel everywhere. It was the days of powdered egg and ration books.

Televisions were only owned by a few, and although the first transmissions took place in 1936,they were to all intents and purposes a rarity. The Harris's weren't to get one until much later.

All the kids within the area took gas masks wherever they went. They used to call them Mickey Mouse masks. Terry recalls that they were part of your school uniform.

Terry's first school was Duddon Hill. It was a mixed school catering for infants right the way through to senior level. The school itself wasn't too bad, but Terry really didn't seem to care to strongly for it. During the many bombing raids, the children were all taken to the communal shelter beneath the schoolyard. This also doubled as a classroom, and lessons continued as best as possible and when time allowed. Terry recalls how they all felt safe down there, and after school some of the more daring boys would return to the playground to use the shelter as a den. The school never knew and anyway no harm was done. Camaraderie amongst the kids always prevailed. They all knew just how lucky they were to be alive.

Terry still had mixed feelings about the school. He had discussed with Winnie and Bill the possibility of being moved to another school. The surrounding area didn't lend itself to this idea, what with the distance involved, but after a visit to the headmaster, it was agreed the he could continue his schooling at St. Marys. Terry looked forward to the change, but found that the school wasn't really any better than the first and making new friends wasn't that easy. Within weeks he was back at Duddon Hill and there he was to remain until his schooling was over.

People say the best days of your life are at school. As time went on, Terry was to for the most part enjoy his schooldays. There wasn't much to think about but the next bomb. It was on his mind constantly.

The teachers lived up to their names. Terry recalls that Mr Stribling sounded just like his. Ted Owen was the only one that the boys got to call by his first name. Most art teachers seemed to be easy going and he was no exception. He used to insist that they called him Ted. There was only one female teacher at Terry's first school a Miss Kitson. None of the kids really took a shine to French that honour going to 'Jean' Wingham. Most schools contain a bit of a masochist and in most schools it was always the master who took gym. Mr Butler. it didn't matter if you were fat or thin if it was up the ropes then up the ropes it was!

As Terry grew older he like the rest of the boys would move towards the rear of the school hall. The older boys used to play all sorts of wheezes during assembly just to get out of the first lesson. A favourite was to speed up the hymns. Terry's headmaster Mr Dolding could never understand why the singing of such simple hymns could go so wrong. He would stand on the platform waving his arms frantically. After three or more false starts he would decide that enough was enough and kept the 'culprits' behind for extra hymn practice! Most of the masters knew what the wheeze was and were to be seen quite often enjoying the fun behind his back!

As time progressed Terry moved further up the hall. His desk mate was a young lady Marianne Davies. She apparently wasn't too keen on him. Later when he became famous, she visited the Palladium to watch him perform with the Shadows. She must have had a change of heart for a short time after she became his girlfriend. Terry's first ever classmate was Sylvia Flindall. Being only five at the time they sat next to each other during class.

Most schools had one teacher who used to generalise. Terry's was no exception. Miss Kalin seemed to fit that bill. Terry who wasn't that keen on school would sometimes end up going walkabout. On one occasion he was out of luck and Miss Kalin ended up tying him to his desk with raffia. Terry together with another old school friend Alan Hazeldean got their own back on her one-day by urinating into this stuff, which hung in the corner of the classroom. Needless to say the stuff was soon removed!

Music lessons didn't really amount to much. They always seemed to be the first lesson. Nobody had to really learn much during this period it was a case of just sitting around and listening.

Assemblies invariably through up the odd mishap or two. The boys who were fortunate enough to use a fountain used to fill up the rubber tube with water. They seemed to make a really good water pistol. Terry remembers during one assembly he had promptly filled his before his entrance to the hall. Safely concealed within his trouser pocket all would have appeared to be well. Not quite it burst! It looked to all and sundry that he had wet himself!

Safety first was always the priority of the day. With the war still going on time was invariably split between the classroom and the air-raid shelter. By 1945 the war was over. The greyness that had surrounded London suddenly lifted. Within a matter of weeks the rebuilding had begun. London was coming alive.

Terry had been at school some eighteen months or so and to him it had seemed to have flew by. During those dark dank years of the war, holidays were virtually out of the question. School holidays apart, a visit to the seaside for any kid was a bonus.

Winnie and Bill had always had a lot of affection for the

Isle of Wight, having spent many happy years there before the Second World War had started. Winnie had always maintained that it was a very romantic place, and the pace of life compared with London seemed to suit them both perfectly.

For Winnie and Bill it was a time to renew their love of the island. For Terry it was to be his first holiday. Terry had never been on a ship before let alone crossed any stretch of water apart from the river Thames! The ferry to Shanklin gave Terry his first glimpse of the sea. The size of the boats in and around the Solent filled him with wonder.

Terry recalls that his first ever memory of the island was barbed wire. Although the war was over there was still a lot to clear up. The beaches were lovely...a far cry from the ruins of London.

A Mrs. Douglas ran the guest house. She was a round-faced lady who always had a smile for everyone whatever the weather! Terry recalls his first ever seaside breakfast perched high on a cushion on one of the old oak chairs that arrayed the dining room. Being knee high to a grasshopper didn't lend itself any favours when eating at a big table. The rooms were always spotless, especially the linen cupboard on the upstairs landing. Whenever it was opened it wreaked of mothballs! A big gong would sound twice a day for breakfast and evening meal.

The summers in those days always seemed to be full of sunshine. The days on the beach seemed to go on forever too. Rock pools took up most of young Harris's time, carrying every known species up the beach in his bucket, especially crabs! He was to encounter something similar later in his life...

Those holidays will always hold a special memory for Terry.

Terry like most boys in the forties was into football. Terry had always loved football and although there were many great sides in and around London he had no personal preference. Bill wasn't really a football man but would encourage Terry all he could often kicking a ball around on the beach for what seemed like hours on end. Terry had always dreamed of becoming a professional footballer, but size plays a part and to be honest he wasn't the tallest thing on two legs! Terry reckoned that Bill was the best father anyone could have wished for.

The main family interest was speedway. Winnie and Bill followed the Wembley Lions watching such idols as Bronco Wilson and Billy Kitchen. The trip back on the underground from Wembley Park Station always ended up with a bag of chips!

Wrestling too took up some of the family time. Wembley Town Hall the venue. Favourites such as Jackie Pallow, Steve Logan, and Mick McManus were all starting their careers around this time. Terry's particular favourite was Les Kellett. Les was a showman through and through. He would fake a roll off the ropes leaving his opponent grasping at thin air!

The only sporting hobby that Winnie and Bill did together was cycling. On fine days especially weekends, Terry would often be found perched rather precariously in a little seat behind Bill as they pedalled off to the park.

Terry's early childhood seemed to be dominated by football. That's all everybody did at school. He looked forward to playtimes. Some of the boys would try and smuggle out the odd big ball from the school hall, which like most schools doubled as a gymnasium. No end of balls seemed to be disappearing onto the school roof or sailing over the school wall never to be seen again.

Although Terry had visions of becoming a football star, his real interest in sport never materialised until his progression into senior school. During the transition to senior school, Terry's work progressed steadily. By today's standards, his work wasn't too bad. His writing though was a different story. It left a little to be desired and judging from his school reports didn't seem to be getting any better.

Terry really hadn't a great deal of interest in music. The early days for Winnie and Bill consisted of a wireless. They were into the big band sound, and apart from traditional jazz, there wasn't a lot else going on. Winnie and Bill also enjoyed the old time music hall, probably due to Vesta Tilley being one of Terry's distant relatives. They were both keen followers long before Terry was born. Saturday night was always variety night. Terry remembered with affection trips to the Metropolitan on the Edgware Road. All the greats were there...Max Miller, Nat Jackley, and Tommy Handley from the

ITMA gang and one of Terry's all time favourites, Jimmy Wheeler.

To Terry the music halls were days of innocence. Those days are long gone. Nothing has replaced them. The closest one has today is the end of the pier show and even sadly now they are on the way out. The old timers are dead and gone but the barrel of laughs that they left behind will never be forgotten. The usual fish and chips followed carrying away what seemed like a mountain of chips for fourpence (1.5p). There always seemed enough to feed everyone!

The Metropolitan was one of the finest theatres in London. Steeped in history. The stage seemed enormous and like most old theatres had an orchestra pit. The music was live in those days, no backing tapes for those guys. Terry was fascinated by the conductor who stood at the front waving his baton thinking...I could do that. Terry recalled that there were no more than about six or seven in the band, and the double bass player seemed swamped by the size of his instrument for he was small too. A little later Terry was to make his first ever appearance on that stage.

Like most boys of that age, he joined the local cub pack in Willesden. Apart from the usual tying knots and the like, they were asked to put on a play. Terry landed the part of a police inspector. The play was to be shown at the Met.

Winnie and Bill attended the performance. Terry who always suffered from nerves before a performance recalls things looked a little different from up there! He was to appear there again along with Larry Page as one of the Page Boys, but probably more famously along with Cliff.

This early appearance seemed to fire his imagination. Winnie and Bill had never really been into music or acting in any way, but Terry was quite taken by the idea. The only musical member of the family that sprang to Terry's mind was his uncle Nobby. This man could get a tune out of anything! Terry used to chuckle with laughter during the many visits to and from his aunties, watching Nobby get into some weird instrument or other.

The front room of his Auntie Sis housed a piano. When left to his own devices, he would often be found tinkling on it, it was pure fascination. Terry remembered the regulation aspidistra that stood beside the leather chaise lounge. Every house must have had them!

The back room of his aunties contained a large black range. Everything of any importance seemed to find its way onto it, from boiling water to the pot of stew! Gas mantels were the order of the day; electricity wasn't standard in every house. Nobby and Sis lived about six miles from Willesden in Southall a 105 bus being the mode of transport.

Nobby and Sis always made Winnie Bill and Terry welcome, and port and lemon was always available. Terry would on occasions partake of the odd one or two whenever they stayed over. Terry recalled that on occasions he would sneak down stairs and help himself, returning to drink it beneath the bedclothes! The drinks never affected him perhaps it was due to the gripe water that Winnie had bottled fed him with that it had no effect!

Terry's schooling continued. As he got older the knocks got harder. His sporting encounters not only included the usual football and cricket, occasionally hockey was the order of the day. According to Terry this game is not as simple as it might appear, for during one of these games he received a rather nasty blow to the head with a stick. The player didn't mean to hit him but neither did Terry, when he returned the compliment with a rather less than friendly crack to the shins! His school cap hid the lump!

Terry had reached the age of ten. Holidays continued across the Solent. His dreams of becoming a footballer were getting stronger. The young girls in his life were only schoolmates, but he was to fall in love during one of his visits to Shanklin with a young lady Frances Westmoor. She originated from Ryde and Terry remembered her big brown eyes and her long brown hair. Frances was a year older than Terry, and they used to meet up every day and walk hand in hand to the beach. Winnie and Bill must have chuckled at them holding hands as they paddled about in the water!

Roller-skating took up part of their holiday. You've either got it or you haven't. Terry and Frances were both naturals. Terry recalled that a glass of pop and a bun were the order of the day after a strenuous skating session.

The first girl who really caught his eye lived just around the corner from the family home. Susan Green was a pretty little thing. Holding hands at the Saturday morning matinee Terry and Susan were both 'Ovalteenies'. It was the days of the Saturday morning sing-a-long with songs like "I've Got Sixpence", the bouncing ball above the words on the screen. Most cinema managers of the day would read out the birthdays from the stage. Terry remembered how the cinema managers all looked the same in those days. They always dressed in penguin suits and all had the obligatory pencil thin moustache! Their local manager looked as if he only owned one suit, a real shiny arse!

One Saturday Terry and Sue were sitting there watching the main film. Suddenly without warning, she turned to him and planted a big kiss right on his lips! Terry wondered what the hell was going on! He remembered thinking...

"Christ, it scared the bleedin' life out of me!" Mind you it didn't the next time...He gave her one instead!

Every school had its exhibitionist. There was always a girl who would show you hers if you showed her yours. Some of the boys did not. Terry was to remain a virgin until he reached eighteen years of age. Everything was so innocent in those days. Nobody knew anything about the birds and the bees.

The teachers at Terry's school were hard but fair. There were some you could enjoy a laugh with, whilst others would think nothing of throwing a board rubber in the direction of your head as soon as look at you. Every school also had its fair share of bullies. Duddon Hill was no exception. Paul Hickey was a hard little bastard who always seemed in but there wasn't a light on. He was the sort of kid who would hit you just because you were there.

Being a mixed school gave the boys all sorts of opportunities to put one over on the girls. The toilets were a constant source of amusement. A wooden fence separated the toilets being situated across the playground. Some of the taller boys could actually reach over and flush the girl's lavatory whilst the young lady was still sitting there! The teachers knew what was going on. If you were caught it meant the stick from the headmaster. Some boys were gluttons for punishment and kept going back for more. Not Terry. Anyway, he was too small to reach over!

Kids these days seem to have no respect for anything or anyone. Terry recalled, in those days if you felt the rough end of the stick you didn't dream of going home and telling your mum and dad for fear of getting another one! Bill wasn't a violent man, but if a smack were warranted, then a smack it would be.

The Saturday morning matinees were a place to muck about. When there was a good western on some of the Boys would dress up as cowboys, the full Monty, hats and guns, the whole schmozzle. Terry remembered how they would sit there and shoot their guns at the baddies on the screen. Terry's favourite was Flash Gordon and everybody's favourite baddie the Emperor Ming. Of course like everybody else, Terry would go back the next week to see if Flash had survived the onslaught of Ming's special army!

The balcony provided the ideal place to really cause havoc. All sorts of wheezes went on. Bottles of fizzy pop and stink bombs would find their way to the stalls below, all hell breaking loose whilst the recipients tried to explain that it must have come from the balcony and had nothing to do with them!

The cost of admission was sixpence (2.5p). It was the days of Palm Toffee and the Archie Andrews lollipop. Some of the boys used to try their hand at smoking the odd cigarette that they had purloined from some place or other. Most of the culprits would usually end up in the toilet, throwing up after inhaling the smoke. Bill used to smoke. Winnie didn't like it, but just put up with it.

Suddenly the years had gone. Terry was now approaching school leaving age. On occasions he couldn't wait to hear the school bell. Academically, Terry wasn't the brightest of pupils. Winnie and Bill encouraged him to try for a course at the local technical college. After a lot of hard work and help from his parents, he managed to gain a scholarship and enrolled for a course in Art and Building.

The course lasted a year. Terry took up the challenge with great relish. He had something to prove. The course itself was an education. It was the easiest one on offer. Terry recalled, there were lots of free periods during which he and a few others would slope off into the music room to try a few instruments. His only involvement with music up and till then was a paper and comb! Music seemed like hard work to Terry, the thought of all that practice. out of the question. Now art?.. that was a different question!

Art classes were fun, especially the life classes. Some of the models were to say the least a little past their sell by date! Terry often wondered if that's how all women turned out in the end. Luckily all of them didn't!

Terry seemed to possess an artistic flair for something, even if it was playing around with a few bricks and pots of paint. Being much older and stronger although still small, he interest in sport became more intense. He was still kicking a ball around and being a non-smoker enabled him to stay reasonably fit. He was picked to represent the College football team. Playing at outside right and having plenty of pace, seemed like good credentials for being spotted by one of the many scouts who would attend games all over London, searching for new talent. In swinging corners was Terry's speciality. He kept his place and would end up with about eight or nine goals at the end of the season.

Terry continued to play week in and week out hoping for that break. It never came. Athletics also became part of the curriculum. Terry tried his hand at the long jump, but decided he would concentrate on the 100 and 220-yard sprints. Running seemed to be what he was best at.

Athletics did run in the family. Winnie had already competed at the White City before he was born. Both Winnie and Bill had visions of him becoming another Chris Chataway who ran probably the most memorable race ever seen at the stadium. It was televised and having purchased a television they all sat around watching the white searchlight following Chris and Emil Zatopek on that epic last lap.

Terry's speed too had won him many races. He was beginning to gain quite a reputation. He was quite nippy, but once again couldn't quite make that extra step into the big time. He did however; manage to be selected, as first reserve for the all London schools Athletic meeting in 1953.Running became part of his daily routine. He would run to college and back, timing himself at every opportunity.

He was running everywhere.

Terry was getting noticed, especially by people at the college.

They used to say...

"That Harris, Christ he flies like a Jet!"

The name seemed to stick. So Jet Harris it was...

School Reports

COUNTY COUNCIL OF MIDDLESEX.

BOROUGH OF WILLESDEN EDUCATION COMMITTEE.

DUDDEN HILL SECONDARY MODERN BOYS' SCHOOL

Report for ....

Name .... Form ...... No. in Form ......

Age at end of term ...... Average age in Form ...... Times absent ......

Scale of Marks: A = Well above average. B = Above average. C = Average. D = Below average. E = Well b

General Remarks

Conduct ....
Diligence ....
Progress ....
Helpfulness ....

Form Master/Mistress ....

Headmaster/Headmistress's Assessment

Has worked well this term. A very helpful boy.

.... Headmaster/Headmistress

22

School Reports

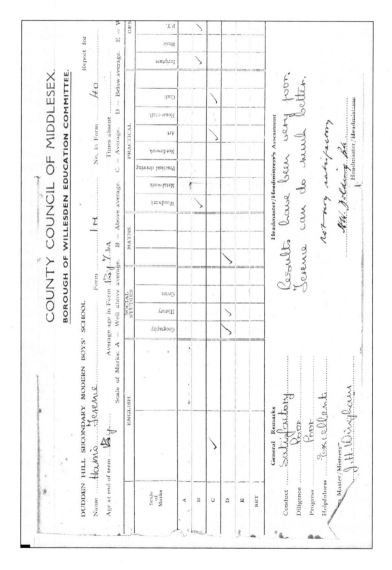

School Reports

COUNTY COUNCIL OF MIDDLESEX.
BOROUGH OF WILLESDEN EDUCATION COMMITTEE.

Report for Autumn Term, ending ....

Form .... 2 A ....   No. in Form .. 35 ....   Position in Form ..... 9 ....

Average age in Form ..... 12¼ ....   Times absent ....   No. of times late ....

Marks: A = Well above average.   B = Above average.   C = Average.   D = Below average.   E = Well below average.

Headmaster's Assessment

Next term begins .... 9 JAN. ....

Next term ends .... 9 APR. ....

24

School Reports

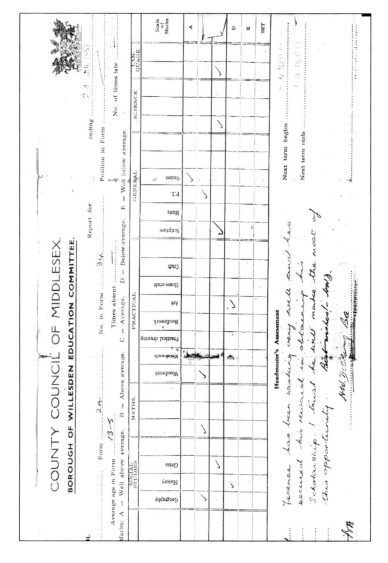

The Young Ones...

The music of the early fifties much like the forties, was dominated by the big band sound. Vera Lynn the forces sweetheart was still actively making records, having retained some of her popularity from the war years. A signing for Decca, her first three recordings Auf Wiedersehen (10), Forget Me Not (7) and Homing Waltz (9) gave her success. Forget Me Not re-entered the charts giving her her highest position at number 5 for the next two years, all the recordings charted between the 14th-19th November 1952. Vera had to wait those two years for her only number one, My Son My Son. Vera like so many others came from the big band era. The only competition if any seemed to come from Jazz.

New Orleans is reputedly and lovingly known as the "Mother of Jazz". For many people, Jellyroll Morton led the way. Jelly was born in 1890 and his style to say the least at times a little obscure. His genius wasn't really recognised until much later in his career, dying in 1941 virtually penniless.

Until that moment in his life, a young Jet Harris who was approaching sixteen hadn't really taken much interest in music. He remembered the charts being dominated by such stars as the Stargazers whose hit I See The Moon reached number one in 1954.They had already reached number one the previous year with Broken Wings.

Many people were influenced by the big band swing orientation none more so than Doris Day whose song Secret Love reached the top in April 1954.The song was probably more remembered when recorded by Kathy Kirby in 1964.The song that stuck in Jet's mind was Doris's recording of The Black Hills Of Dakota which seemed to be playing on the radio everyday.

Other stars who always on the radio during that time were Johnny Ray with Such A Night, and Miss Kitty Killen with her recording of Little Things Mean A Lot. There was no doubt in Jet's mind about the most successful star that went to Frankie Laine. Frankie's first twelve recordings all make the top twenty. He had two consecutive number ones with Hey Joe and Answer Me. Winnie and Bill were both into the Big Band Sound. Being raised during the Count Basie and Louis Armstrong era counted for a lot. Their music like that of Glenn Miller is still as popular today as it was then.

Teenage years are renown for periods of misspent youth. Jet was no exception. There were days when he would just idle away the time bit he was slowly becoming aware of music. As a nation there were stars to match the Yanks. We had Eddie Calvert(The man with the golden trumpet).There was Vera of course, David Whitfield and a man that Jet was to become great friends with the late Michael Holiday in 1958.

Jet recalled, looking back on those days everything was so exciting. He reckoned that there is only one man who has made more comebacks than him Frank Sinatra! Frank's first number one Three Coins In The Fountain in 1954 seems a long, long time ago and to find him still charting in 1986 with Theme From New York New York reaching number 4 is success by any standards.

The country as a whole seemed ready for a change. There was a feeling in the air that something was about to happen. The war was well and truly behind everyone, people were beginning to find their own niches. The music of the fifties seemed to lift everyone.

Apart from mucking around in the music room at school, Jet's only real involvement with music was during his last term at school. Paul Jenkins, a class mate of Jets used to play a pretty mean piano. Most schools had one person who could play and Paul was no exception. Jet spent many nights after school listening to him knock out the odd tune here and there. Paul's speciality was boogie. His left hand work was something to be admired. Jet was fascinated. He could only dream of playing like that. Jet did in fact ask his mum and dad if they were prepared to let him take piano lessons, but however much he pleaded with them, it was out of the question. Money was still tight.

If Jet Harris owed anything to anyone it must be Paul. His influence on his later career was to prove enormous. Paul had planted the seed. It was time to take up the challenge. The next two years of his life were to be dominated by music. He began to eat and sleep music. He was desperately keen to play something, but the price of musical instruments was out of the question. It was down to him.

Jet took up odd jobbing even doing a paper round to raise as much money as he could. The 4/6d (22.5p) he earned by today's standards wouldn't have bought an awful lot, but every little helped. Winnie and Bill were impressed with his endeavours, so much so, that they offered to help him all they could. With other money coming in from chopping wood and cleaning windows he managed to scrap together a tidy sum. He couldn't afford a piano so he bought the next best thing...a clarinet!

Unlike a piano, a clarinet didn't take up too much room, and being determined to succeed he began to practise. To Jet the mundane routine of playing his scales night after night seemed boring, but if he wanted to play music he must first learn to read it. Jet recalled that playing boogie on a clarinet is a little different to a piano!

Jazz seemed to be the only outlet for clarinet. There were a lot of bands around in the fifties. Jet was suddenly listening to them all. One of the British bands at that time were The Dixielanders who had formed back in 1943. Wally Fawkes played clarinet. Wally was to join Humphrey Littleton who having left the army in 1947,after reaching the rank of captain, had decided to form his own band.

Jet was gleaning anything from anywhere. Breathing techniques were most important, listening intently to how and when to blow. The number of bands to choose from seemed endless. Chris Barbers New Orleans Jazz Band, The Crane River Jazz Band, Alex Welsh's Jazz Band, you name it he listened.

Bill unlike Winnie encouraged Jet all he could. Winnie was a little more sceptical, she really didn't fancy the idea of her son getting involved too deeply with Jazz. The seedy clubs in and around Soho that Jet was to attend held no appeal. Although only sixteen coming on seventeen, Jet had visited a few drinking parlours which featured jazz. The landlords got to know him and he nearly always got in despite being small in stature. It was during this period that he became hooked on something else. Tobacco.

Everything in those days seemed to revolve around a packet of fags. Jet had tried the occasional fag during his early visits to the pictures. He was determined to give it a try. It seemed the sociable thing to do. Smoking has never done Jet any favours.

For Jet it never came to picking up dog-ends in the street that was to come later. His health was to suffer some years later. He was soon hooked and in no time smoking when money allowed quite frequently. Winnie and Bill never knew. Jet had always been slightly asthmatic, and smoking didn't do a great deal for his breathing. He was suddenly having trouble finding the right breaths for his clarinet. After six months he decided to stop smoking.

For Jet, the clarinet had given him an inroad into music, but he still yearned to play boogie like his mate Paul. Winifred Atwell was the nearest thing that Jet had heard since hearing Paul's playing. Now Winifred's left hand playing was something else!

Winifred had the unique distinction of being Britain's only black female piano player. She was never out of the charts. Her career stretched for nearly eight years. Her first entry Britannia Rag stayed for six weeks, reaching number 5 in 1952. Releasing records in those days wasn't a problem. It was nothing to have five or six records out in any one year. Her follow up recordings all made the charts. Coronation Rag, Flirtation Waltz and Lets Have A Party (made number2) in December 1952.

A string of hits followed all making the top ten. She finally made it to number one with Lets Have Another Party in November 1954 and Poor People Of Paris in March 1956.No matter where you were her records was always being played. Jet was even more determined to play boogie. He had wasted what little money he had on cigarettes. He was still odd jobbing along with his work with his father and perhaps in hindsight that money would have gone a long way to paying for piano lessons.

Within a couple of months Jet had saved enough money to trade in his clarinet for a battered old double bass.

He had remembered all those years back at the Metropolitan watching the bassist never thinking that he too would end up buying one let alone playing one! He knew this move would enable him to play boogie. The local music shop had had this monstrous thing in the window for sometime. He took the plunge and went in and bought it. It took some carrying home!

Jet paid around £30 for it and recalled the look on Winnie and Bills face as he carried it into the sitting room! Never mind getting out of breath playing the clarinet, He was out of breath carrying this bloody great thing even before he had attempted to play it! He knew instinctively that he had made the right choice. Once again it was down to practice and practice he did. With the rudiments of music all ready there, he soon got into it. Winnie and Bill wouldn't allow it in the sitting room so the bedroom became the practice room.

With the aid of an old gramophone he began to acquire all the Winifred Atwell records he could. Winnie wasn't the only piano player he'd listen to, but she was more accessible and easier to play along with.

Practice makes perfect and soon Jet had become quite a dab hand. His visits to the clubs were to increase as he progressed, but sadly for him he was to drift back towards cigarettes. He was still getting out of breath occasionally, but he didn't seem to care. His job as a sheet metal worker had given him money, but he felt that he really wasn't cut out for factory work.

Jet had still kept in touch with his old school mates.

Two of them, Pete Newman and Geoff Wickens were both well into jazz. Both were saxophonists and were heavily into Charlie Parker.

Charlie Jnr. 'Byrd' Parker was a master. Born in Kansas City on the 29th August 1920.Charlie's early influences were towards the development of 'Bop' in the forties, and he had worked at both the famous Minton's Playhouse and Monroe's Uptown House in New York.

Charlie entered hospital in June 1946 due to a nervous breakdown, mainly induced by his addiction to heroin and alcohol. He stayed in hospital until January 1947. His life was to say the least a little torrid having tried to commit suicide on two occasions, mainly due to his bad debts. His last public engagement was at the Birdland nightclub New York on the 5th March 1955. He died some seven days later.

Although his style wasn't of a purist nature, his improvisation was rooted firmly in traditional jazz. His best known being 'Anthropology' based on chord progressions of Gershwin's 'I Got Rhythm' Pete and Geoff who had never seen Charlie perform used to eat sleep and drink his music. They both had visions of becoming famous. Jet had until that time only been listening to purist music, mainly traditional. That was soon to change. He was to discover Charles Mingus.

Charles Mingus Junior was born around the same time as Charlie in Negales, Arizona on the 22nd April 1922. He like Jet had toyed with a few instruments before settling on the double bass at high school. Charles was to become his mentor. Winifred Atwell suddenly seemed an age away and yet she was still making records. Jet began to read up on Mingus. It was to stand him in good stead for the future visiting jazz clubs. It would give him something to discuss.

Mingus had studied under Red Callender, a former bass fiddle player with the New York Philharmonic, touring with many bands as a guest player throughout the forties. He spent a year with Barney Bigards Ensemble before gaining attention with Red Nervo's Trio along with Tad Farlow in 1951.Charlie Parker had played with Mingus on many occasions towards the end of the forties early fifties.

Mingus spent most of his life in America. The nearest that Jet ever came to seeing him was a little later during the sixties when he made one of his only appearances on British television on Jazz 625. Mingus became so successful that he formed his own record company, Debut Records. His contribution to the Jazz Composers Workshop during 1953-55 produced some marvellous improvisation.' Ladybird' rated as one of his best.

Another great piano man who was once Charlie Parkers sideman was the legendary Thelonius Monk born in Rocky Mount, North Carolina on October the 10th 1917.He like many others had also played at Minton's but had never recorded anything in a studio before 1944,playing with The Coleman Hawkins Quartet. He had had a spell with Dizzy Gillespie's Orchestra before finally recording under his own name in 1947 on the Blue Note Label.

Monk was becoming a regular word around the jazz clubs. He signed a three year contract with Prestige Records releasing his first solo album in 1954.Monk like Mingus and Parker, didn't establish himself until the mid fifties.

He died in Weehawken on the 17th February 1982.

Jet remembered that all three had a great influence in their own way upon his career. With so many avenues to follow Jet had visions of forming a band. Another old mate of Jet's Ray Edmunds who played drums, offered to sit in with them and give it a try.

The four young men took to getting a few tunes together. It seemed to work. For obvious reasons they used each other's houses. Although Winnie and Bill were into swing, they didn't really want to hear it every night above their heads! Most of the sessions would end up just sitting around drinking the odd beer and smoking the odd cigarette. The boys were to remain friends for many years and for Jet, it would be another thirty years before he would again meet up with Pete Newman in the production of 'Some Like It Hot' in the mid eighties.

When they weren't playing, it was the jazz clubs. London had many. Ronnie Scott's, The London Jazz Club at Mac's Rehearsal Rooms in Great Windmill Street near Piccadilly and the Caribbean Club in Denman Street to name a few. The clubs weren't that easy to get into though the more seedier ones seemed more accessible.

Winnie and Bill must have had nightmares about Jet hanging around these places. Soho was more renown for its strip clubs and smoky back street bars. It wasn't what Winnie or Bill for that matter had wanted for him, but Jet being so young and positively headstrong didn't leave them with much choice. If mistakes were to be made along the way then so be it. Terry recalled "there always seemed to be a guardian angel watching over him".

Jet was becoming more independent. His trips to and from Soho took about half an hour by tube. Carrying his double bass proved quite a problem especially up and down the escalators! He didn't need to take the bass with him every night only on the ' free and easies' .He would just sit around talk and listen to jazz. He was learning. He was beginning to get noticed. He wanted to be part of it. His wish was to come true.

An audition followed with Don Lang of Six-Five Special fame, for a string bass player. He passed. Geoff and Pete were both thrilled for him and wished him much good fortune. Jet was still living at home, and Winnie and Bill somewhat apprehensive about a forthcoming tour gave him their blessing. During his time away, he would try and send home a little money to help them out. Jet stayed with Don for a few months. Terry Dene an up and coming singer had offered Jet a chance to play with him. Terry was a very likeable guy and seemed destined for big things. Sadly he never fulfilled his true potential, only scratching at the surface of the industry. When Jet later joined The Shadows in 1957 Terry's song 'A White Sports Coat' reached number 18. The King Brothers had all ready recorded it in May of that year their version reaching number 6. Terry's career was short-lived. His next two releases Start Movin' (15) and Stairway To Love (16) giving him two more top twenty hits before he faded from the scene.

Jet's time at the jazz clubs was to prove invaluable. Jet felt that he must give credit to one of the most respected bass men of that era, Sammy Stokes. It was Sammy who took Jet 'under his wing' teaching him an awful lot. Sammy played with Ted Heath's Band alongside the likes of Kenny Baker (Trumpet) Jack Armstrong and Don Lusher (Trombonists), Scott and Johnny Gray (Saxophonists), and drummers Jack Parnell and Ronnie Verell.

Sammy was also featured on a package tour with Oscar Peterson in 1955. Along with drummer Tony Kinsey and Ella Fitzgerald. His track record spoke for itself. Sammy taught Jet technique, presence and most of all gave him the confidence to go forward and on to better things.

America was producing a new sort of music, Rock 'n' Roll. Elvis was about to hit the scene with Heartbreak Hotel hitting the charts in May 1956. Because of the success of his first recording, Elvis released a further eight singles including Blue Suede Shoes, Hound Dog, and his first number one, All Shook Up. Within twelve months.

Jet recalled that Britain too was producing its own fair share of Crooners. Ronnie Carroll 'Say Wonderful Things To Me' (1963) and Roses Are Red (1962) and his first recording back in 1956 Walk Hand In Hand on the Philips label reaching number 13.Another Ronnie, Ronnie Hilton had been having hit records since 1954. He only managed one number one in April 1956 hitting the top with No Other Love.

The Americans led by Nat 'King' Cole were making a strong headway into the British charts. Nat had fourteen singles in the top twenty between 1952-1956.He like many singers to follow never had a number one. He reached number two three times with Pretend (1953), Smile (1954), and the classic When I Fall In Love in 1957.

Elvis apart, British popular music was still in its infancy. Jet recalled although there were plenty of talented musicians about, no one had taken the bull by the horns. The Americans were again about to kick start a new generation. Bill Haley was about to hit the scene.

Bill and his group The Comets had recorded Rock Around The Clock from the film of the same name. The song had actually been written in 1927 and was to be a smash hit some thirty years on. It was to reach the top on its second attempt in October 1955. Bill had already released Shake Rattle And Roll earlier in December1954 reaching number 4.Critics said it wouldn't last. Bill was to prove them wrong. His next six records all made the top thirteen over the ensuing fourteen months.

The ground had been broken and the scene was set.

Jet recalled that all Britain really had going was the Six-Five Special and Cool For Cats. We had Jack Jackson, Charlie Chester, Pete Murray and Jo Douglas. The purists still had their jazz, but for Jet the transition into this latest wave of music was to be his swansong. He didn't really know where it would end but he was going to play a very important part of it in the years to come.

Jet stayed with Terry Dane until early 1958. Lonnie Donegal and Chas McDevitt were all making their own kind of music. The meeting place of most of the muso's was the legendary Two "I's" coffee bar at number 59,Old Compton Street, in the heart of Soho. Many famous names were to pass through its doors, Adam Faith, Marty Wilde, Tommy Steele, Cliff Richard....

Jet recalled that Central London was the place to be. Soho to him was more like a miniature Harlem, seedy clubs, and ladies of the night! All the musicians in and around Soho seemed to pull for each other. When they weren't working they would just hang around the bar on the off chance that a gig might materialise.

The Two 'I's' became a musician's Mecca. Young players would come from all over the country in the hope of being 'discovered'. The Tommy Steele story saw to that! It was the 'in' place to be.

Jet recalled that Soho itself was a very colourful place. The smell of oriental food was always in his nostrils! It seemed to lend its own aura to the place. The people too were a breed unto themselves. Soho being a 'red light' district meant the occasional visit from the law, but generally there wasn't really any trouble. Everybody kept themselves to themselves. Jet could never remember seeing a miserable face. Everybody always seemed so happy. It was just like a continental village. True it had its fair share of 'shady' characters, but it really was the place to be.

Jet recalled that the Soho fair took place every summer. The streets were packed with entertainers, carnival floats, buskers; you name it they were there. The whole place 'ceased' trading for the day. The waiters had their own special race. They would run along the street carrying a tray with a bottle of wine and glasses precariously set upon it. They were good days. It was to be the first time that Jet managed to get 'stoned' out of his mind!

Jet had gained a bit of a reputation as a bass man. Wally Whyton used to frequent the bar and during one of these visits he got talking to Jet. Jet jumped at the chance of joining him and duly became one of The Vipers. The original group consisted of Wally, Jet and a really weird guy named Johnny Booker. Johnny used to go by the name of 'Zom'. Jet later discovered that he had acquired the name because he looked like a zombie!

Jet's first recording was with The Vipers. Summertime Blues/Liverpool Blues on the Parlophone label was to be their only single. A young Tony Meehan had sat in on a session some months before joining The Shadows, along with Wally and Johnny. Wally had all ready recorded with The Vipers Skiffle Group earlier in 57.Lonnie Donegan also had a cover version of Wally's Don't You

Rock Me Daddy'O and Cumberland Gap. Lonnie taking the latter to number one as against Wally's number ten.

Jet remembered that during one of those early sessions with Wally, history was nearly made. Wally had suggested playing a few instrumentals. The producer, a young George Martin sat and listened to this sound that Wally had come up with. Wally had been experimenting with putting echo on to his guitar. The result was incredible. George liked it, but because his work took up all of his time, he was unable to advance it any further. None of the boys either ever got around to doing anything with it either.

The sound was to become synonymous with The Shadows.

The Vipers could have been The Shadows!

The Two"I's" was originally called the Three "I's", being run by three Iranian brothers. One brother left and then there were two. The bar had become quite famous and due to the many people who wanted to get in a small charge of one shilling(5p) was made at the door.

Jet recalled that the bar itself never catered for any unruly types. A doorman who went by the name of 'Lofty' used to keep an eye on the clientele also taking charge of the money. The room itself wasn't all that big. Musicians would just get up and play when they felt like it. Paul Lincoln who was managing Terry Dene and Wee Willie Harris at the time, took charge of the acts.

Wee Willie Harris is, as Jet liked to point out, not his little brother!

Most of the action took place in the cellar. Jet would try to play most nights. Bruce and Hank had played with Jet during one of their early gigs at the bar. Tony Meehan also put in the occasional appearance. His time was mainly spent taking it all in. Tony was still at school and although still young had become a regular face at the Two "I's".

The Vipers used the cellar regularly, playing mainly jazz/skiffle. Skiffle had been the rage for some time, and many clubs in and around Soho were catering solely for that purpose. Russell Quay ran a club in Greek street featuring The Worried Men. Terry Nelhams was the main singer who later went on to become Adam Faith.

Another popular haunt was Studio 51 just around the corner from the Two "I's". Lonnie Donegan and Chas McDevitt were leading the charge, Chas running a club in Berwick Street known as the Freight Train. Chas together with Nancy Whiskey took the song of that title to number 5 in April 57 staying in the top twenty for seventeen weeks.

The success of the two "I's" had sparked off a revolution. Clubs were springing up all over the place. No matter what the others put on, the Two "I's" was always number one. As Jet recalled, the sign above the door said it all..

HOME OF THE STARS.

Jet used to call it the Black Hole Of Calcutta! It had been decorated by one of Britain's earliest 'beatniks' the voyeur Lionel Bart. The cellar didn't lend itself to any ventilation. People would pass out nightly not from exhaustion but from the heat. Jet recalled that there was never any jealousy between them. Everybody was keen to make progress. They were all good in their own right. a stable full of future stars.

Jet's first amplifier came via Clem Cattini of Tornados fame. offering to lend Jet the money to purchase one. Clem recalls that he told Jet to pay me back when you become famous...he never did...pay him back!

To Jet, the nights seemed endless. You would often find yourself drifting around the corner to yet another bar with live music. Nobody ever got paid at the Two "I's", it was all for love.

Across the water in America, a young teenager was making a name for himself. James Dean was the teenage image of America. He was beginning to influence a lot of young people in Britain. James Dean was the sort of person that Jet could associate with. He was small. Jet was small. He decided that an image change could do him no harm.

For Jet there was no half measures. He decided to dye his hair blonde and much to Winnie and Bill's amazement added the secret touch to make it glisten.. Vitapointe! Returning to the bar the impression had done the trick. This was the 'new' Jet Harris.

Work was a matter of being on call. If you weren't there someone else would step in for the night. The Vipers still earned a little and Jet spent most of his on beer and cigarettes. The Vipers had become quite popular so much so that Wally was offered a residency at the bar. Wally had worked for a time at the Breadbasket and although the money seemed like peanuts the residency would give Jet the opportunity to leave his bass at the bar. The cellar wasn't always packed. Jet recalled that on some occasions Paul would have to take the hat round to keep them on a weekly retainer.

Success was just around the corner.

Jet had divided his time between home and a flat-cum-basement in Eccleston Square, Victoria. Jet shared with Wally and any muso's who happened to be in the area that came looking for a place to get their head down. Hank and Bruce had stayed over occasionally. Wally and Jet had a menagerie of animals in the flat. Two monkeys one called Elvis and the other called Higgins. Under one of the beds they kept a skunk called Sam. Sam didn't smell, he had had his stink removed! It didn't stop there for down in the cellar they also had a fox called Sandy! They had for good measure at one time even kept a bear!

From time to time The Vipers would be called upon to gig a little further a field. Jet recalled gigging somewhere around Stoke-On-Trent. The transport was an old American car, a Metropolitan Nash. The show had finished and they were loading their equipment back into the car when Johnny Booker who according to Jet "could be a little vacant at times" reversed the car straight over his guitar!

Another story that came to mind during one of those long hauls involved a young Tony Meehan. The journey took them past a field of sheep.

Johnny turned round and said to Tony...

"We've been on the road for some three weeks now, and we haven't seen a woman. We're getting a little desperate Tony, What I want you to do is this. Jump out here (they were in the middle of nowhere) and go and get us a sheep!"

Well the silly bugger only jumped out and tried to catch one! Tony returned to the car some ten minutes later declaring that they were too fast for him!

Jet remembered another show that they were doing possibly up near Bradford. Another group of old friends were appearing just down the road from them. Johnny Duncan and the Blue Grass Boys. They will always be associated with the single hit Last Train To San Fernando which reached number 2 in July 1957. The night before the gigs, the guys had all met up for fish and chips and a general night of inebriation on the local cider. Johnny and the Boys took a bit of a shine to it and continued to drink it on the night of the gig.

Disaster struck!

The unique mixture of the cider with the food had given Johnny a bit of a problem. The two bob bits! The boys in the band laughed so much that they suddenly began to suffer from the same fate! Sounds incredible but its true. How does Jet know this?... During the interval and after a change of clothes Johnny came down to tell them..

It had only happened to Jet and Johnny Booker that same night also on stage!

Though money wasn't flush it didn't pose a problem when it came to drinking. Jet had now begun to take quite a shine to his beer. It never affected his playing and his body had by now become quite used to it. The travelling to and from gigs gave his system time to recover.

From time to time other guys would drift in and out of The Vipers, guesting when they were in town. One character Jet did remember was John Vanderbosh. He was by far one of the weirdest people he had ever met. One minute he would be up on stage giving it stick, the next back in the dressing room often to be heard singing "I wanna die I wanna die!"

Jet too guested on occasions. Larry Page who was known in those days as The Teenage Rage gave Jet a few gigs, Jet becoming one of his Page Boys!

The coffee bar was still attracting a wide variety of musicians, not only pop but jazz too. Jet happened to be there one night when a guy called Tony Crombie happened to call in. Tony had spent some time playing drums with Geraldo and his Orchestra. Tony used to frequent the Club Eleven along with many other muso's, Ronnie Scott, Tommy Whittle, Jack Parnell, Laurie

Morgan and Johnny Dankworth. Tony had spent most of the late forties just 'jammin' around. He had hosted Accordion Club for the BBC Light Programme, playing alongside Pete Chilver, Joe Muddel and Ray Ellington.

Tony was one of the first Bebop drummers and took in many tours, including one featuring Annie Ross. During a tour in 1954, Woody Herman commissioned Tony to write some arrangements for him. Tony's credentials were immaculate. He approached Jet and offered him a position with his band. Jet jumped at it. They seemed to hit it off right from the word go. It was during this time that Tony invited Jet to look at a new fan dangled contraption he had seen in a local music shop. Little did Jet know this was to become his trademark.

A Framus Electric Guitar had arrived from America. Jet took a look and thought yes, I'll have a bit of that! The shop in Charing Cross road no longer exists and Jet to this day believed he had held the distinction of owning the very first electric bass guitar in Britain. Things were really about to change.

Overnight he was suddenly in full demand. Everybody wanted to see this thing work. Electric guitars had been around for years, but no basses. Jet's income suddenly rose dramatically. So did his smoking and his developing interest in liquor. To be fair to Jet, all muso's would get a little 'tight' every now and then, but his attitude towards alcohol wasn't to get any better.

Winnie and Bill still kept an active interest in his chosen occupation, although Winnie still wasn't happy. He had chosen this as his career and as long as he was happy she was prepared to let it go.

Soho was crawling with women and Jet had yet to lose his virginity. He didn't have to wait too long.His first sexual encounter took place in the flat of an Indian lady. Zeta worked as a nurse at the local hospital, frequenting the coffee bar on her nights off. Jet had noticed her, but up until then, hadn't really given it much thought. They got talking and she took him back to her flat. According to Jet, it was all over in seconds. He never even made first base! Zeta must have known this and after a few more visits and a little more practice he was up and running!

Tony Crombie was affectionately known as 'the governor' and it was on a tour with Tony that Jet really lost his virginity! Wee Willie Harris was also on the same bill. Jet was to fall 'in love' with one of the dancers on the show, Doreen Lovidge.

Jet recalled that they were playing real theatres in those days, with real stages. He was now on the princely sum of £18 a week. Doreen earned only 6.10 shillings (£6.50). She was beautiful and always smiling. As the tour progressed they began to get on quite famously. All of their spare time seemed to be spent together, even keeping in touch after the tour for some years to come.

The tour had opened Jet's eyes to the pain that the dancers went through. Doreen would come off most nights with splinters in her legs. Part of her routine was to finish off with the Can-Can. The audience were completely unaware of what these girls were going through. Jet spent many nights back stage removing the splinters form their legs. Doreen like the rest of the girls had to buy their own stockings getting through so many pairs tore a small fortune from out of their salaries. They all shared the same room to save money although bed and breakfast and evening meal didn't cost anymore than about £2 per person per week.

Most of the acts at one time or another stayed with Mrs Mac. She was a dear old lady who ran a guesthouse for artistes in Manchester. Nothing was ever too much trouble for her. The famous and the not so famous were all treated the same. She always ensured that all her guests were well and truly fed and set up for the day.

Jet was now beginning to drink a little more each day. Tony used to keep it from the rest of the band, Jet recalled as long as he performed on the night, Tony would turn a blind eye. Mrs. Mac didn't allow anyone to drink in her house. She ran a tight ship. Jet had craved for a drink some nights, but he knew the rules and he abided by them. The likes of Mrs. Mac are few and far between these days. Jet remembered her with great fondness and respect.

The Tony Crombie tour ran for weeks. To Jet it seemed endless. London seemed miles away. The Two "I's" good or bad had given Britain the kick-start it had needed. No matter wherever the touring muso's where, the coffee bar was always regarded as home base. Although Jet had all ready played alongside Bruce and Hank, The Drifters still weren't in sight.

Jet recalled that many of the artistes were suddenly here and gone. This went for the Americans too. Sal Mineo, with Start Movin' (1957), Tab Hunter who reached number one that year with Young Love and Fabian who three years later with Hound Dog Man all faded within weeks. Britain had its share too. Johnny Duncan, Chas McDevitt, The Kalin Twins and Jerry Keller who had a one hit number one a couple of years later with Here Comes Summer.

Making records wasn't as technical as it is today. The Shadows recording of Apache being completed on a Vox four track machine. Musicians did it 'live' in those days. It was down to raw talent and sheer determination. you only got out what you were prepared to put in.

The Crombie tour was over and it was back to home base, the coffee bar. The experience that Jet had now under his belt was immeasurable. Mickey Most another up and coming muso had heard of Jet's ability on the bass guitar and offered him a position with his tour. The pay was £31 a week, and although the tour was only to last for three weeks it seemed like a good thing to Jet, so he accepted. It was now 1958.

On the bill was another act. Cliff Richard and his group The Drifters. They were a new outfit and unlike Jet were virtually new to the game. Cliff had recently changed his name on the advice of a bar owner in Ripley, Harry Greatrix. Cliff had been gigging in and around London for sometime albeit in a small way. He had been spotted and had in fact signed a recording deal with the tour went well. Cliff often standing watching the other acts perform. He seemed to take a shine to Jet and his playing. and was keen to talk to him.

Jet remembered him saying,

"How nice to meet you Mr. Harris, would you consider coming to work for me?"

Jet told him that he would have to think about it and left it at that. Jet recalled that Cliff was very well mannered. He had the looks and looked like a good bet for success. "Move it" had just been released in August of that year. "Schoolboy Crush" was actually the A side, but those that went out and bought it, thought that "Move It" was the song destined for the top.

Jet watched with interest as the record climbed the charts. Everybody kept in touch with the music business by buying the musical papers of the day. For some it was an ego trip, seeing you name in the What's On guide served as a kind of fame. Cliff had all ready had a fan club created by life long friend Jane Vane. By the time the record hit the charts there were some 10,000 members!

Groupies had always been associated with the Beatles. Jet recalled that it was no different in those days. All the groups had their fair share. With Cliff's record doing so well, young ladies would flock to see him. Cliff unlike Jet was always protected from them. Jet was now no stranger to women and when the opportunity arose he would naturally accept it!

Cliff's record continued to climb reaching number 19 in the first week of the tour. By the end of the three weeks, it had hit number 2. Jet spoke to Cliff, and agreed to join his band.

Jack Good was one of the most influential people on the British music scene. Jack produced probably TV's best known show since Top of the Pops, Oh Boy!. Cliff had already been lined up to do the show, and it wasn't going to be too long before Jet himself was to appear.

It was go for a couple of Jet's other friends, the late Dave 'Screaming Lord' Such and Adam Faith. Dave was a kind and gentle man During the mid fifties Jet and Adam got on really well together. Some days you had money other days you didn't. Jet remembered vividly how the two of them were really brassic one day and how they had managed to 'cadge' five shillings (25p) off a fellow muso. Having not eaten a real good meal for two days (Their money had gone on beer and fags!) they left the Two 'I's' one day and shot across the road to the Act 1 Scene 1.a small cafeteria almost directly opposite the coffee bar. They ordered two of the biggest plates of spaghetti Bolognese you could have ever wished to see! They stuffed theirselve's stupid!

Hank and Bruce still popped into the coffee bar every now and then. Hank was fast becoming the best thing around on guitar. Hank hadn't got his famous Stratocaster then, he used a right monstrosity, an old Antora guitar. Hank said it did the job.

Hank and Bruce had all ready joined Cliff in the interim

period replacing Norman Mitham and Ken Pavey both rhythm guitarists in October 1958.Cliff was also playing guitar, and on Bruce's arrival decided to concentrate on his singing. Jet had replaced Ian Samwell in that same month. By July of the following year1959, Tony Meehan was to complete the line-up.

Cliff's new group had come a long way from The Quintones, Cliff's first band. Terry Smart who drummed for Cliff, felt that he couldn't commit himself totally and Tony was eventually drafted in. Terry had had a little success drumming for the Dick Teague Skiffle Group before joining Cliff.

Jet was no stranger to television. He had appeared along with Don Lang on a show earlier in his career. Although he had worked with Don on this occasion he was part of a group known as Le Hobo (The Tramps) led by a guy called Les Bennett. Les ended up with Lonnie Donegan and is probably best remembered for The Chewing Gum Song.

The industry then as today, had its share of gay people. There doesn't seem to be any stigma attached with it today. Jet was surrounded by gay people who never used to bother him at all. It never stopped him from enjoying their company. Soho catered for all races and all creeds, it was a tight community.

Jet remembered with affection some of the great gay characters. Old 'Maude' what a fella', totally harmless.' Second Hand Rose' always accompanied himself with a bottle of champagne. Whenever you walked past she would often be seen standing in shop doorways shouting...

"You German bastards!"

Jet recalled that everybody was German when 'she' hit the bottle! She even went the whole hog, shaving off her eyebrows and pencilling the buggers back on!

'Iron Foot Jack' and old Iris Orton who used to wander the streets in a long black cloak! Jet felt that he might have been easy prey especially with dyed blonde hair (and a dash of Vita Pointe!) but they never bothered him.

Eighteen months had now passed since his first tour. His income had increased dramatically, but drink and the craving for cigarettes had eroded it. The one or two drinks that he used to enjoy with friends, were now creeping up to six or seven. But he still did his job, being totally able and competent to perform at the drop of a hat. Jet didn't feel that he'd got a problem with anything. He would keep himself in fairly fine fettle. Playing was all that mattered.

Had his introduction to Gripe Water by Winnie all those years ago orientated him towards alcohol?... only time would tell.

Soho was not only a meeting place for musicians but also gangsters. The coffee bar had been taken over by a couple of Australian wrestlers, Doctor Death and Rebel Ray Hunter. They could handle themselves, and any trouble that might have occurred, quite easily.

The bandwagon was about to roll. For Jet the next few months were to be hectic. Jet was well and truly going to be a part of it. The stopper had already loosened its ugly head from the bottle, and that aside all he could do was go with the flow.

The stable of artistes was now full. the Two "I's" had seen to that. Marty Wilde, Billy Fury, Shane Fenton(Alvin Stardust) and newcomers, Jess Conrad and Mark Wynter were now knocking on the door. Jet seemed to have been around forever.

The year he had spent working with Tony Crombie and Wally Whyton had given him tremendous street credibility. He had something to live up to. Nerves have always been apart of Jet's life. For some people they are never apparent, but in his case they will always there. His ability to perform was never in doubt and any 'edginess' prior to a show was soon calmed with a couple of beers.

Tours were hastily arranged and completed via an old Bedford coach, with little or no heating. Cliff and the boys would literally eat sleep and 'drink' in this old thing. Being one of The Drifters didn't mean an automatic rise in pay, in fact Jet's wage stayed about the same. Bonuses came in the form of the odd Television spot with Cliff.

John Foster had taken on the mantel of moulding the group that had been formed to back Britain's answer to Elvis. Jet admits that with the greatest respect to Terry,

Norman, Ken, and Ian, they didn't really match up to what John had got in mind. John had found Hank and Bruce, Hank only agreeing to sign up as long as Bruce could. Hank with his Buddy Holly glasses had impressed John for some time. Hank had the ability to lay good solo pieces and this had impressed John greatly. Hank might not have made the group if John had heard the original guy he had come to hear Tony Sheridan...but luckily for Hank Tony was nowhere to be found.

The Mickey Most Tour had put Jet firmly in the spotlight. Ian 'Sammy' Samwell had left to concentrate on song writing and managing the group. John and Cliff had both approached him offering him the position. Hank, Bruce, Tony and Jet, the line-up was complete..

Life would never quite be the same again....

CLIFFHANGER....

December 1958. The winter was upon them but however cold the winds were to blow that year, for four young men and their singer, the temperature was about to rise. The group had changed beyond all recognition. They looked and sounded like a team.

John Foster had taken on the mantle of moulding the group that had been formed to back Britain's answer to Elvis. Jet admitted that with the greatest respect to Terry, Norman, Ken, and Ian, they didn't really match up to what John had got in mind. John had found Hank and Bruce, Hank only agreeing to sign up as long as Bruce could. Hank with his Buddy Holly glasses had impressed John for some time with his ability to play good solo pieces but even Hank might not have made the group if John had heard the original guy he had come to hear -Tony Sheridan. Luckily for Hank Tony was nowhere to be found!

Eighteen months had now passed since Jet's first tour. His income had increased dramatically, but drink and the craving for cigarettes had eroded it. The one or two drinks that he used to enjoy with friends, were now creeping up to six or seven. The year he had spent working with Tony Crombie and Wally Whyton and The Mickey Most Tour had put Jet firmly in the spotlight, giving him tremendous street credibility but now he had something to live up to. Nerves had always been a part of Jet's life and now any 'edginess' prior to a show was soon calmed with a couple of beers. He still did his job though, being totally able and competent to perform at the drop of a hat. Jet didn't feel that he'd got a problem with anything. He would keep himself in fairly fine fettle. Playing was all that mattered and the bandwagon was about to roll.

For Jet the next few months were to be hectic and all he could do was go with the flow. Tours were hastily arranged and completed via an old Bedford coach, with little or no heating. Cliff and the boys would literally eat sleep and 'drink' in this old thing. The new Drifters first appearance with Cliff was at the Manchester Free Trade Hall in January 1959. The show was compared by an up and coming comic from Liverpool, Jimmy Tarbuck. Jet's old boss Tony Crombie and his Rockets were also on the bill along with Jet's other old mate, Wee Willie Harris.

Being one of The Drifters didn't mean an automatic rise in pay though, in fact Jet's wage stayed about the same. Bonuses came in the form of the odd Television spot.

Tony was the youngest member of the group. Born

Daniel Joseph Anthony Meehan on the 2nd March 1943, Tony had attained his first drumming position at the age of 13, spending some time as a member of the London Youth Orchestra. Jet and Tony got on quite well during their Viper days, and it seemed the natural progression to end up working together. Jet had spoken to John Foster about him, and had in fact persuaded John to offer him the position.

Hank 'B' Marvin as he has always been known was born to a Mr and MrsRankin of 138 Stanhope Street, Newcastle-Upon-Tyne on the 28th October 1941. Hank was christened Brian Robson Rankin but was called Hank from an early age. Hank took his surname from the American singer, Marvin Rainwater.

Bruce was born on the 2nd November 1941 in Bognor Regis, the only son of Stan Cripps and Grace Welch. Bruce took his surname from his mother who sadly died two years later.

Hank and Bruce had met whilst attending Rutherford Grammar School, spending time together playing locally in a skiffle group, known as The Railroaders. Wherever music was you seemed to find Bruce and Hank. They would enter numerous talent contests together, eventually entering one that took them both to London. Because of Hank's glasses, (he couldn't see ten feet in front of him) he was easily recognisable for bearing a passing resemblance to Buddy Holly.

Cliff was born on October 14th 1940 in Lucknow, 'British India' to English parents, dispelling the rumours that he is Indian! India was still part of the British Empire and early life for Cliff was fairly comfortable. The movement towards Independence was to change that though and after a short time he and his family returned to England. Life wasn't as easy in England, with his father becoming unemployed for a short while so to help, Cliff stayed briefly with his grandmother in Carshalton then with an Aunt in Waltham Cross before returning to the family in a move to Cheshunt after the arrival of his sister Joan. Cliff's education didn't quite match up to his families expectations. Failing to reach Grammar School, he completed his education at the local Secondary Modern. Cliff, like Jet, had always been sports-minded but he also developed an interest in acting and music. The music of the day always seemed to be coming from Radio Luxembourg, and no doubt, like Jet, he must have listened in regularly.

Cliff's idol was undoubtedly Elvis. Cliff had actively been involved with skiffle, as had Jet, but Rock 'n' Roll was his preference. Cliff, like Terry Smart too, had performed with The Dick Teague Skiffle Group but Jet felt that Cliff always wanted to be like Elvis.

Cliff and the original group had done the odd showcase to secure work and had impressed George Ganjou who was at the time promoting a talent contest at the Gaumont, Shepherds Bush. George suggested that they demo their music and send it to Norrie Paramour, a record producer with EMI. It was Norrie who asked Johnny Foster to recruit a better guitarist, prompting Foster to go to the Two "I's" looking for Tony Sheridan and finding Hank!

On this label, before Tony joined, Cliff Richard had recorded 'Living Doll/Steady With You' with Jet, Hank, Bruce and original backing group member Terry Smart which reached number 20. Feelin' Fine/Don't Be A Fool (With Love) and a follow up Driftin' backed with Jet's own composition Jet Black were released by the Drifters in their own right in January and June of 1959 but didn't really do anything.

Tony was installed in February and in April the completed line up were back in the studios at Abbey Road. Cliff had been rehearsing for his first film Serious Charge, due for release in May and The Drifters were to record the soundtrack for the movie. For the Drifters and Jet it was to be their first experience of the film business. Jet had always thought how romantic and thrilling it must have been to be on the big screen but reality was a different thing. The expected thrill didn't materialise, especially if you were on call at the crack of dawn.

John Foster was managing the Drifters but Franklin Boyd had been installed as Cliff's new manager since October 1958. It was John who secured their contract for the Oh Boy! series. Cliff had already appeared on the show that September. The producer was Jack Good, one of the most respected men in the business and Oh Boy! was the launch pad for the many household names of the day. Jet appeared alongside Shane (Alvin Stardust) Fenton and the Fentones, Marty Wilde, Tommy Steele and the late Billy Fury. Jet recalled that Billy was a lovely man never seeming to have a cross word for anybody. He managed eleven top ten hits, but never made the coveted number one spot.

For Jet the pace of life was beginning to increase. It wasn't unusual to be recording one minute and then doing a spot on television the next. Most of the TV work was on Oh Boy!, going out live on Saturday night without a backing track in sight! They were mobbed everywhere they went, especially Cliff. Those in the know were grooming him for stardom.

Jet recalled that Cliff's father who had always had a vested interest in his son's career, dismissed both John Foster and Franklin Boyd shortly after Tony joined and this opened the door for the new man, Tito Burns.

Tito, who took over in February wasn't too happy about the name. Jet recalled that they for some time been confused with the American Drifters who had acquired the name before them. The American Drifters had nine top ten hits, and like so many others, they too never reached number one. Cliff had already released his first EP and with the second one about to come out something had to change. Names come and go, but they were about to come up with one that would be written into the history of popular music for all time.

Jet recalled that he and Hank had ridden out to Ruislip one day. It was the days of Lambretta scooters and Mods and Rockers. Mods were always associated with scooters and although they were never either, Hank, Bruce and Jet all had one. They had their chauffeur driven cars but it was much easier to commute across the city on one of these. Jet went everywhere on it. They stopped off for a drink at a pub called The Six Bells and over a couple of beers Jet and Hank sat discussing the name change. A few names were thrown around when Jet suggested the Shadows. It had occurred to him that they were always standing in the shadows behind Cliff, so why not use it. Hank agreed, It sounded right. They jumped back onto their bikes and raced back to tell the others.

Unbeknown to Jet at the time was the fact that Bobby Vee had also used it for his backing group before he became famous. That group had split up now so there was nothing to stop them using it. The others fell for it straight away, so Cliff Richard and The Shadows...That was it.

The name change meant that contracts had to be altered, and this was duly done in February 59. By this time the schedule was getting hectic. Cliff's film had placed him firmly in the spotlight and a second film Espresso Bongo was already being talked about with a possible release in September '59. Something had to break and as Jet recalled it did...Cliff lost his voice! Cliff's father hastily stepped in and cancelled any immediate work for Cliff and he soon recovered.

Making records wasn't as technical as it is today. Musicians did it 'live' in those days. It was down to raw talent and sheer determination and you only got out what you were prepared to put in. Technology has come on in leaps and bounds since those early days. Back then it was common practice to have an old wind-up gramophone. Radiograms and the eternal Dansette complete with an electric stylus were also fast becoming popular...no more changing needles!

December 1959 saw The Shadows first release under the new name. Saturday Dance/Lonesome Fella on 78rpm stayed just outside the top thirty. The disc synonymous with the sixties, the 45rpm was in production and it wasn't long before all recordings were completed and released on these smaller discs. The Shadows sound was about to hit the country. Hank had been given a guitar as a present by Cliff. The American Fender Stratocaster, Hank still uses it to this day. Suddenly every group in the country seemed to be using them. Eric Clapton, Mark Knopfler, Hendrix, Holly, they all used them. Hank was Mark's idol and his guitar playing stands as testimony to the instrument in question. As a group The Shadows all used Fender guitars and Vox Amplification. Shops up and down the country were doing a roaring trade. A sum of £375 or so would cover the cost; an arm and leg for most muso's at that time.

They travelled everywhere, just getting their name and sound out there. Jet even appeared in his first pantomime, completed in December 59. An American tour taking in around thirty shows the length and breadth of the country was next. Jet recalled that during one of the many tours that were to follow, the coach driver turned up late at a theatre in Bradford. *"The fans, some three thousand or so, had been waiting, some time for us all to arrive. Chanting had started and they started the show some two hours late."* A couple of weeks before, fans had tried to smash down a door at the Blackpool Opera house in an attempt to get in. Cliff and The Shadows were invited to appear on a Royal Command Performance in May, along with Russ Conway, Lonnie Donegan, Adam Faith and the legendary, Nat 'King' Cole. The Shadows were becoming popular.

In early 1960, it all nearly came to an end when Jet and Hank had a nasty car accident just outside of Stockton. Jet who was driving (and on this occasion thankfully completely sober), was in a head on collision with another vehicle, swerving across a greasy road to miss one and hitting the other. The cars were a total mess and luckily for everyone, the only thing seriously hurt was Hank's glasses. The show went ahead that night, with sticking plaster holding them together! Neither of them had a license and the courts didn't find it very amusing, taking rather a dim view of the whole incident. Jet was fined £3.15 shillings (£3.75) for dangerous driving, having no 'L' plates on the vehicle and driving without a qualified driver in the car. Hank for his part was fined £3.00 for aiding and abetting!

The Shadows wanted success and so did Cliff. Jet recalled that Cliff refused to record unless they were all present. Cliff was the boss - he gave the orders. The record labels carried their name, but for the most part they were paid only a session fee for each recording, around £7 a day. The studio time allowed was usually around three hours and Jet recalled that it was nothing to put down three or four tracks in any one session but the recording sessions that took place weren't all wine and roses. Jet remembered that Bruce was always the calming one. *"He seemed to have a lot of influence over Hank. They had always been the best of friends but to hear them row sometimes, you wouldn't have thought so! They used to row like crazy, but we all did. There wasn't a leader as such, we all came up with ideas, and perhaps that's why it worked."*

The Shadows desperately wanted a contract of their own. The royalties from their previous recordings didn't amount to much, most of the money going to Cliff. They wanted to have success in their own right and managed to secure a contract with Columbia Records. They were all under 21 so Jet, being the oldest, took that responsibility although his father had to come in to sign as a sort of guarantor.

The contract with Columbia was to be worth only four records, with no guarantee of any being released so it didn't seem to be worth an awful lot, but to Jet it was a step in the right direction.

With all this new found 'fame' and attention Jet began to drink heavily. He was still in control but he remembered that Bruce, who was teetotal at that time, didn't really approve, and their relationship became strained. Their aims and ideals still remained the same regardless and throughout the whole period Jet had a lot of respect for Bruce. He was a perfectionist. He above anyone seemed to keep them all on the right track. Whatever water has since passed under the bridge, Jet still held him in high esteem. He regards him as one of the finest chord men in the business. Bruce had the ability to create highs and lows, light and shade. He knew when to lift the music and when to calm it down. Jet admitted that Bruce was right; he did drink too much. Jet would think nothing of going out of the studio straight into a bar. It was easy come, easy go.

The man with the overall say on those early sessions was Norrie Paramour. Any disagreements over the chording, he would be down to sort them out. Jet got on well with Norrie; not only was he one hell of a good record producer, he was also a really nice person. With Cliff he knew just what was required and with Norrie's invaluable input Cliff and The Shadows were to achieve no less than eleven top ten hits including five number ones between 1960-64. Jet, Hank and Tony never lost sight of the fact that they were ordinary blokes who just happened to stumble onto a winning formula and tried not to let it go to their heads but Bruce had suddenly become a little 'aloof' from the rest of them. He seemed to have the air of 'look at me, see what I've achieved'. Mind you, Jet said that they all used to take the piss out of him from time to time.

Cliff on the other hand was a different matter. Jet remembered that, although he worked with him, Cliff didn't seem to mix with them as much as he might have done. Not only was he protected from the general public, he appeared to be protected from The Shadows. This did not detract from the fact that Jet reckoned regardless he has remained to this day what he was then, a genuine person.

Over the next two years, as success took off, a great many changes were to come. Cliff changed his manager again with Peter Gormley taking control. George Ganjou, who had originally spotted the young Cliff's undoubted talent, had sold his remaining promotion rights to impresario Leslie Grade and Expresso Bongo, Cliff's second film, was set to be released. Once again it was crack of dawn time for Jet. The early morning calls didn't do him any favours especially if he had had a rather 'heavy' night before. He'd be longing for a beer by mid morning.

As a group the Shadows were still under contract to record for Columbia and were still waiting for that elusive hit. They had recorded 'Saturday Dance/ Lonesome Fella' under their new name but this still didn't give them the recognition that they were seeking to achieve. Norrie Paramour was keen to give them that success and called them into the studio to record an old army standard, The Quartermasters Stores backed by a new Jerry Lordan tune...Apache. Although Norrie liked Apache, he felt safer with his original choice so the Shadows entered the Abbey Road Studios in June 1960 to record it. Jet recalled that Cliff sat in on an oriental drum.

They sat and listened to the finished recording. Instantly they knew that Apache was the one. Jet said, call it instinct, they knew they were on to a winner. The record was released on the 29th July 1960 and entered the charts, going straight in at number 17, reaching number one a few weeks later and staying in the charts for a grand total of 21 weeks. Apache lasted less than three minutes but that was all they needed. They had made it. To date Apache has sold nearly thirteen million copies world-wide, making it the most played instrumental of all time.

The Shadows sound was unique. Modern technology has clarified the sound, but to Jet nothing has changed.

A VOX AC30 and a Watkins echo box is all it took, along with Hank's string technique....the way he stroked the strings. The famous 'Shadows walk' was soon to follow. Nobody really had any monopoly when it came to stage presentation, some bands moved behind the singer some didn't. Jet remembered that none of them were too adept at fancy footwork so they kept it simple but Jet did admit that they had somewhat 'nicked' the walk from another band that had toured with Jerry Lee Lewis but it has since become theirs, and became legendary. Even Cliff was doing it!

Apache gave the Shadows more independence. They were now established as a group in their own right and didn't have to rely on Cliff, not that they did anyway, and during the next eighteen months hit was to follow hit.

November 1960 saw the release of their new single' Man Of Mystery/The Stranger' which reached number five, spending 15 weeks in the charts. 'F.B.I./Midnight' soon followed. Hank, Bruce, Tony and Jet wrote it under assumed names. It gave them their third top ten entry, reaching number six and staying for 13 weeks. May 1961 gave them hit number four. 'Frightened City/ Back Home' climbed to number three and remained in the charts for 20 weeks. The second number one came in September. The haunting tune 'Kon-Tiki' backed with an original Jet Harris tune 36.24.36 stayed around for 10 weeks. During this period the worst position came from the release of 'The Savage/Peace Pipe' which only made number ten and an 8 week chart stay!

Alongside this they were still recording with Cliff,

featuring on no less than nine more hit records including two number ones. 'Please Don't Tease/Where Is My Heart' and 'I Love You/'D' In Love'. Jet recalled that they were never out of the charts.

This independent success meant that firstly, when touring with Cliff they were able to open the first half of the shows, then later they were able to tour on their own. Jet recalled, *"it was life in the fast lane all right, I just looked forward to sitting down after a show, preferably in the nearest bar"*. Jet had kept in touch with Winnie and Bill, sending them the odd postcard and when in London popping over to see them. They too would reciprocate by coming out to see him perform whenever time allowed.

Bands all over the country were imitating them and their music. Since the arrival of Hank's Fender (Bruce still had the same one some thirty five years on!) the shops were now full of them. Jet's position and career had taken on a whole new meaning. Everybody wanted to play like the Shadows.

Not all the gigs went smoothly. Jet recalled playing the Chiswick Empire. Some of the more unruly lads in the crowd thought it would be good fun to throw a fire extinguisher from the balcony into a crowd of screaming girls below. Pandemonium broke out. Jet recalled that the only time in his career that he could remember leaving the stage before they had finished their set was at the Lyceum, just off the Strand. They were being pelted with fruit and coins. They looked at each other and said..."That's it" and they were off.

Success had given him a niche but it was still a learning process for Jet. He was comfortable but the ride down the helter-skelter had got faster and he felt like he needed something else apart from the safety of the bar.

With the constant travelling there wasn't much time to take on a steady girlfriend but Hank had one, Billie, and Bruce had taken up with a young lady called Anne. Jet remembered pulling in for petrol one day in 1959 at a garage in Hounslow. The young lady who served him was Carol Costa. Jet fell in love at first sight. He remembered that she had those Bridget Bardot-ish looks. Carol had recognised Jet from television and newspaper coverage. Packing in her job, she decided to tag along with Jet and before you could turn around they were married. Jet remembered that her parents were two of the nicest people you would ever wish to meet.

Jet and Carol seemed perfect. Their courtship was to say the least, a little whirlwind but Jet was totally besotted by her.

Their wedding in June 1959 was attended by two 'best' men. Daley and Wayne had been on the same bill as Jet at the London Palladium, where Cliff and The Shadows were playing that season, and he had asked them to officiate. Cliff and Tony were both away at the wedding, they had gone to Italy. Jet recalled Tony telling him that he purchased a packet of condoms whilst over there, opening them up in front of Cliff. Cliff left the room and promptly threw up. Tony had told Jet that they had made Cliff feel quite sick!...in short, he thought they were awful things!

Carol was to go everywhere with Jet, but as Jet was to learn later, the only reason she married him was to be near Cliff, a fact that Jet confirmed. Carol openly admitted it to him a long time after. During this time, the shows at the Palladium went on nightly. Jet recalled some of the antics that the dancers used to get up to. Most of the male ones were gay and remembered his dresser telling him of a conversation that he had overheard between them regarding him. It went a little like this…"You see that little one, the blonde one, umm she's on drugs umm!"

Apart from the odd joint Jet had never taken drugs. He admitted that he didn't need to he had his own personal supply at the bar! In fact drink was never far away from Jet. Many nights he could be found at the bar, putting even more down his neck. Tony would sometimes join him for a quickie, but he knew when to stop. Carol had managed to get a job working behind the Palladium bar so he didn't have to worry about her safety. After all she was his wife and at the end of the night she was going home with him. Carol had already told Jet that she liked Cliff, but so did every other young lady in Britain. They were at an age of slight innocence, everybody was still so young. Jet still really wasn't cottoning on that Carol's attentions towards Cliff were more than friendly. Carol played her part well. Jet recalled that there were many rows, but they always ended up back together.

Jet and Carol had set up home in Streatham but most of the time they could be found around Cliff's. Cliff had purchased a flat at No 100 Marylebone High Street. Jet recalled that it was pretty spacious and, working mainly at night, it just meant somewhere to crash out during shows. Hank who lived in Finchley would often entertain Jet and Carol too. The choice of flats gave them a chance to avoid any untoward visits from fans, being in different places meant that they were difficult to find. Cliff had three sisters, and on occasions Donna the youngest one would drop in for a cuppa. Donna was just out of school and Jet thought, "She's going to break a few hearts along the way."

Most of Jet and Carol's spare time was being spent flitting between their flat and Cliff's Marylebone flat as it was fast becoming a commune. Musicians would drop in from time to time. Jet recalled that there was never a dull moment as there would always be something to talk about. Like the time Carol stayed home and Jet, away in Worcester received a panicked phone call. Elvis the pet monkey who was still with them, had escaped onto the roof and had begun to throw slates into the street below! After a short discussion with the fire brigade, he was eventually rescued and returned to the flat.

Most of the time Carol would accompany Jet on the road. Although becoming slightly wiser, he still refused to accept Carol's interest in Cliff and put it down to infatuation but as the touring went on, Jet began to realise that indeed she was after him. Perhaps his affinity with the beer hid it from him but Jet seemed to be the last one to find out how Carol had felt about Cliff. Cliff had tried to hide his feelings for her, but the sober members of the party were picking things up and began to drop hints to Jet. Jet, at his risk, had ignored the warnings from the rest of the group but now the occasions that he had actually watched them sit goggle-eyed at each other were becoming more obvious. In fact, the affair had started to develop before Jet and Carol had even got married.

He took comfort in the only place he knew...the bar. To Jet, drink was his only friend and he began to drink heavily. Jet said, "You name it, I drank it!" The more he drank the worse it got. Jet knew he was about to lose her to Cliff. Jet recalled that apart from their obvious feelings for each other, Cliff and Carol did try their best to keep it private. They would just get up and leave the room together. Jet remembered Donna turning up one day. She had just turned sixteen, and out of sheer desperation he asked her outright if she would like to go to the cinema with him. "Yes please" she said, and off they both went. Jet recalled that it was all so weird but nobody batted an eyelid. Donna had always appeared so level-headed which for someone so young and having such a famous brother, wasn't easy to do. She seemed to take it in her stride. Jet just didn't want to face what was happening and really began to rely on the bottle. He decided he couldn't put up with it any longer and if Carol could do it, so could he. He had fancied Donna, but an affair with her was out of the question. He began an affair with a dancer he had met during an earlier tour. A tit-for-tat relationship ensued, with her giving him solace when the bottle didn't. She turned up at their flat one day in Streatham telling Carol that she was going to take her husband from her, threatening to spill the beans about the affair. Carol didn't seem to bother.

Later on in life, Carol told Jet that when Cliff and Tony

had returned from Italy after she had married him, the sight of the ring upon her finger was secretly eating Cliff up. Cliff had apparently told Carol how Jet's canoodling with her was upsetting him. The sight of Cliff breaking apart in front of her made her realise that she should have married Cliff. She even admitted that later on, Cliff had asked her to marry him, knowing full well that she was still married to Jet! Carol had talked of the children that she and Cliff would have together. Life was full of surprises and Carol still had one more in store when a story broke in The News of the World, Sept 1990, admitting to having had a termination by Cliff in 1960. During Jet's time with Carol, he could not remember her ever having an abortion and it seemed so unlikely, for neither he nor the rest of the Shadows knew of it either. Cliff and Carol had apparently both pledged that because of their love for each other, they would never marry. Cliff never did. Carol though did find happiness for a short time with someone else.

By mid 1960, for Jet, the marriage was as good as over. He had been married for less than a year. He recalled that it was all he could do to stand up there behind his mate, knowing that he was deeply in love with his wife but suddenly it was all to change. Jet remembered Carol took a phone call (he thinks it was from Tony) telling her that Cliff no longer wanted to see her. Cliff told her later, that he thought it was wrong to sleep with another man's wife. Jet thought that Carol to this day still didn't understand why her affair with Cliff ended. Perhaps the powers that be had a hand in it and perhaps it was the loss of Cliff's father. Perhaps the passing gave Cliff reason to change. Jet recalled, *"One moment it was*

Carol, the next, he had seen the error of his ways". Jet believed that Cliff truly did love Carol. Something told him deep down that it just wouldn't work.

The affair was over but for Jet it was all too late, the damage was done. His life had been turned over but through it all and to his final days, Jet was always fond of Cliff. He loved him like a brother. When all that was going on, he couldn't afford to kick up any dust as he could have lost his job. Looking back he just put it down to life. The whole episode was hush-hush. No one talked about it. Pop music has always had its affairs. Politicians too were 'putting it' about. If you weren't sleeping with the drummer's sister's best friend, you just weren't with it.

In April 1960 a son named Ricky, was born to Carol. Ricky, a shortened version of 'Richard', and was a lovely baby. Jet remembered that Bruce took the call as they were away gigging. "Terry, you're a father" Bruce called out. Jet was ecstatic, but he wasn't really going to get to know him too well for he and Carol weren't going to be an item for much longer. The rest of the boys had their doubts as to whose baby it was and even Jet wasn't always convinced that Ricky was his, and was to harbour doubts for the rest of his life. Confiding in me....

"Who knows, he might not be mine."

The events that had unfolded before Jet hadn't left him much time to think. His respect had disappeared. His respect for life and the people around him was suddenly eroding before his eyes but life had to go on, and once again it was with the help of the bottle. Jet recalled that he had been invited to a party at Cliff's house. Peter Gormley had to take him to one side. He couldn't face it. He just broke down in tears. It had all become too much for him. Through it all Jet and Carol kept up appearances but the drink was making him look awful. Some nights he would look so vacant. The truth was he was pissed. Money wasn't a problem, women, drink. you name it, he could have it. It made no difference.

Jet remembered coming home one night from the Palladium.

Carol's bags were packed. He asked her what she was up to and she told him that she was about to leave with Cliff. He said, "Right, take this with you" and he hit her. Cliff's car arrived outside and off she went. Carol always turned up at the shows alone, never turning up with Cliff.

Jet recalled that it wasn't all doom and gloom at that time though. Life had its lighter moments too. Working in Coventry one night, a beautiful young girl called Gwen had arranged to meet him after the show. Carol by all accounts was still in London, and regardless of the unsettled nature of their marriage, was still his wife. He had arranged to meet Gwen in the foyer when Carol made an unexpected entrance.

Gwen, not knowing Carol, asked if she had seen Jet Harris. Carol being inquisitive and not letting on whom she was asked why, Gwen informed her that she was meeting him after the show., Jet heard her coming down the corridor. She was really blowing.

"Where is the bastard?" she said as she stormed into the room.

"What's up love?" he asked.

Carol began to rant about whom she had just spoken to. Jet extricated himself by telling her that he was only meeting her for an autograph.

Jet said that the affair between Cliff and Carol drove him to the bottle. Everyone who was anyone knew what had been going on with Cliff and Carol. Some say he was a free spirit being totally responsible for his own actions. This is true, but when Jet was fighting what he saw as a somewhat losing battle, alcohol seemed the only helpful replacement.

One morning he woke up alone and looked at himself in the mirror. He remembered suddenly realising that the bottle wasn't the answer. He couldn't hide behind it anymore. Jet for his part had forgiven Cliff, even though the only thing that Cliff ever said to him was, "Sorry mate". So he made the decision to stop drinking. He didn't touch a drop for ages, although by this point, unknown to him, the damage had already been done.

The rest of the group all stood by him, helping him through it as best as they could. Jet remembered Hank saying to him one day that he was best rid of her. Jet said that without his band mates, he wouldn't have survived. Neither Jet nor Cliff ever alienated themselves from each other; far from it; they just carried on as if nothing had happened. It was still a learning process for them all. Jet recalled that one day out of the blue Carol rolled up at Catford. She told Jet that she loved him and wanted him back. His reaction wasn't too pleasant! In no uncertain terms he asked her to leave. Jet and Carol were to divorce within months and he wasn't to see her again for some twenty years. He never saw anything of Ricky his son who was a babe in arms when Carol left. Jet had given Carol the chance to be provided for, she only had to ask. She never did.

Hank and Billie had gone their separate ways as too had Bruce and Anne. No longer with a steady woman in his life Jet's music was his only outlet but life on the road had a way of lightening the moment.

According to Jet, Hank was always getting himself into all sorts of tight spots. Jet remembers one New Years Eve during the Panto season. Hank had wandered off upstairs with one of the chorus girls. The rest of the crew had stayed back for a drink and a bite to eat. Someone commented that Hank had been away for sometime so Jet offered to go and track him down. He eventually found him. She was in a certain state of undress whilst he was banging his manhood on a wardrobe door! He had drunk so much champagne he didn't know where he was!

Cliff too had his moments. Jet recalled that Cliff would be the first to admit that he is not the world's best actor. During the shooting of Expresso Bongo he was called upon to do a very mild sex scene with one of the stars of the film, Yolande Donlan. Being new to the game and still somewhat innocent he was having trouble keeping part of his anatomy under control. He turned to Jet for advice. After a brief consultation Jet returned from a local sports shop with a rather tight fitting jock strap. It did the trick and the scene was completed without undue embarrassment!

THE WORLDS OUR
OYSTER...........

Apart from a short tour of Scandinavia, the flight to America was to be the longest to date.

The American tour kicked off in Montreal. The entourage had flown out a few days before and the whole party were looking forward to a successful tour. The tour was to take in around thirty gigs the length and breadth of the country. The schedule was hectic and there was to be little time off.

Cliff had all ready had some success over the water with Living Doll, the tour being set up to capitalise on that success. Although Cliff has remained a legend in Britain, Jet never understood why he never made it big in the states.

The show went out as The Biggest Stars of 1960.On the bill was Frankie Avalon, Freddie Cannon, Clyde

McPhatter, Sammy Turner, The Clovers, Johnny and the Hurricanes, The Isley Brothers, Bobby Rydell and Linda Laurie and the Crests. A pretty impressive line-up by all accounts. Jet recalled that there wasn't a great deal of time to sightsee, most of it out of the window of the huge travelling bus that took them everywhere. Jet recalled that there really wasn't much to look at - just vast areas of open flat untouched land.

The whole cast seemed to pull for each other. It didn't matter how famous you were it was all hands to the pump! It wasn't strange to see half a bus full of people fast asleep! Jet recalled that there wasn't much else to do.

It was during one of these long hauls across the country, that Jet and Tony were really dying for a beer. The bus had stopped off in some remote town, and it seemed like a good chance to get off and stretch their legs and grab a couple of beers! Tony who was only seventeen at the time didn't realise that the American law that forbade the sale of any alcohol to anyone under the age of twenty-one, and for that matter, neither did Jet. On finding a liquor store they both marched in as bold as brass.

Being British, the Americans always seemed to have a soft spot for tourists, and seemed to get a thrill out of talking to you. Regardless of your age, they would try and sell you anything. On this occasion, the guy behind the counter refused to serve them. Jet and Tony, unlike the owner of the store, hadn't noticed the local sheriff standing by the door! He was intently watching what was going on.

After a brief explanation as to who they were, the sheriff waved them on their way. Jet recalled that they could have both been locked up for under-age drinking. He wasn't the friendliest of guys, but he was only doing his job. Jet and Tony had to make do with lemonade that day!

The heat and travelling conditions had begun to heighten Jet's need for beer. The air always seemed so dry to him and not being one of the world's greatest travellers, would try to sneak one here and there whenever he could.

The Forum, Montreal kicked off the tour on 22nd January 1960.The following day Jet was in New York, Rochester taking in the Community War Memorial Auditorium. There wasn't to be a day off for the whole twenty-nine gigs. Jet and Hank nearly didn't make the flight on January 18th due to a car crash earlier in the month on January 7th.

Towards the end of the tour most of the work was in and around Texas. Will Rogers Memorial Auditorium, Fort Worth kicked off the last week on February 13th, followed by the Sam Houston Coliseum Houston, (14th), Municipal Auditorium San Antonio (15th), Municipal Auditorium, Dallas (16th) and the Coliseum Lubbock (17th). It was during this last show in Lubbock the home of Buddy Holly, that Jet had the pleasure of meeting Mr and Mrs Holly. Jet remembered that they were really humble people. Buddy had been tragically killed the year before, but they still had time for everybody, taking an active interest in the business.

It seemed that everywhere Cliff and The Shadows were to go, Cliff would inevitably end up stealing the show. Jet remembered that Elvis had been called up for military service and was away in Germany. With Cliff 'gyrating' all over the place, the kids just warmed to him.

For all the success of that tour their records never really took off in America. Jet could never understand why, and seemed to have more luck with his accent especially down south! He remembered that they would just put him up against a wall and ask him to talk!

Jet did manage to take in the Alamo during one of the stop off points. The museum is actually built on the original battle site, and houses Davy Crockett's vest (Waistcoat) and Jim Bowies knife.

The earlier gig in New York on the 23rd January to Jet had seemed too big. It was like rush hour every hour. It was virtually non-stop. Sullivan, Ed the leading talk show host of the day invited Cliff and The Shadows to appear on his show. Unlike modern day shows, it was live music all the way on American Television.

One thing that Jet did find disappointing, was Greenwich Village. Jet, Tony and a guy called Mort Schumann went there one night after the show only to find it empty!

Because of the hectic pace of the show, Jet didn't find much time to 'mingle' with members of the opposite gender, recalled that he only had one success during the whole tour with a half Mexican, half Negro girl of exceptional quality!

During one of the long-hauls, Jet struck up a conversation with a guy called Beau, the drummer with the Hurricanes. He suggested that they might go into business together. He asked Jet about the number of Pizza huts back home, Jet informing him that there weren't any. Beau asked Jet to bear it in mind and give it some thought. Perhaps London might have been ready for one. Jet didn't think that it would really take off in England...How wrong he was...The Jet Harris Pizza Huts. The mind boggles!

Like all touring, one lived out of suitcases. Jet soaked up the atmosphere and the general day to day running of the show. He admitted that it was hard work, but wouldn't have missed it for the world. There were many musicians back home who would have loved to have been in his position.

The Shadows returned home and within weeks were back in the studio at Abbey Road. It seemed the norm in those days to put down around ten tracks in a matter of weeks not months like today's hit makers. As a group in their own right, they hadn't yet taken off. Apache was still to come.

A Royal Command Performance was to precede that release. Within weeks Jet was to open at the London Palladium along with Edmund Hockeridge, Des O'Connor, Joan Regan and Russ Conway. The show - STARS IN YOUR EYES.

Jet admitted that after the American tour it seemed like a bit of a come down. Apache was to hit the top during their stay there. They were probably the only group to have a number one record and not be allowed to perform it on any of the shows. They were a little disappointed.

Peter Gurley, an Australian was about to come into their lives. Hailing from Sydney, he had been suggested to them as someone who could safely look after their interests. Jet suggested that they give him a try. Within a year he had replaced Tito Burns as Cliff's new manager.

Hank, Bruce, Tony and Jet were all keen to contribute as much as they could. Apart from their early attempts at writing, they were still pretty naive regarding the recording industry, although they seemed to have old heads on young shoulders. For that reason they decided to form their own music company, Shadows Music. F.B.I. was one of the first tunes that Jet registered, the boys having written it earlier in the flat at Finchley. Peter too is listed as one of the writers. Their names weren't used due to some complications with their previous publishing house. Jet still receiveed royalties from Peter. He never let them down.

The writing bug had got to them. Jet recalled that suddenly they were coming up with all sorts of tunes, Nivram being one of the more famous offerings. Apache had deposed their lead singer from the top of the charts in August. It was to be another year before they released their first album simply called The Shadows. It was at the top of the Album charts within weeks.

Jet admitted that they 'nicked' the Shadows walk from another band that had toured with Jerry Lee Lewis. Even Cliff was doing it. Nobody had any monopoly when it came to stage presentation, some bands moved behind the singer some didn't.

The ladies in their lives led a sheltered existence. For their own personal reasons, they didn't travel too often. Jet has always fancied his chances with the ladies and being in such a privileged position, it gave him ample opportunity to 'experiment'! He was no different to the rest of the boys and if the opportunity arose he would take it.

Jet admitted that people nowadays are more responsible. Aids was no doubt around, but no one really knew of its existence until Rock Hudson developed and subsequently died from it. It was easy come easy go in those days.

Between June and December 1960, Jet was to record a further 28 songs with Cliff at Abbey Road. The season at the Palladium was coming to a close and a rest is really what Jet was looking forward too.

The end of January 1961, again saw Jet back in the studio, putting down a further five tracks in six hours! A mini tour was underway at the start of February beginning at the Birmingham Hippodrome on the 5th. Chas McDevitt and Shirley Douglas along with Cherry Wainer, Dave Sampson and the Hunters were introduced by Norman Vaughan with Cliff and the Shadows topping the bill.

A tour of South Africa was pretty imminent. Jet was due to fly out on March 6th from London airport. The plane was delayed and they ended up watching a horror film in Hounslow! Eventually the plane took off some six hours late. Jet was also down to take in Australia, New Zealand and the Far East some time later in the year.

Their arrival at Salisbury, Rhodesia caused quite a stir. They were met by hoards of screaming girls. Jet remembered "they were everywhere, it was take your pick!" Even the hotel was surrounded!

The tour threw up its moments. Bruce who was still with Anne at the time, ended up on the end of one of Jet's escapades! Jet had happened to have 'had his way' with a gorgeous blonde. Jet recalled that she had bloody great long nails. Hank and Tony were both in on it too. They decided to set Bruce up. Telling him they had a little present for him, Bruce like any other hot-blooded young man jumped at the chance. The state of his back when he returned was something else! How on earth he explained his way out of that one only Anne knows!

Cliff too nearly dropped Jet in it. Carol had long gone and he had a new lady in his life Patti Brooke. Jet had met up with Patti herself a singer during one of the tours. They seemed to hit it off right away. Carol was a thing of the past and Jet's new romance was just what the doctor had ordered. Jet remembered that Patti was gorgeous and her best friend Jackie Irvine had always fancied Cliff, asking Jet if he could introduce her to him.

Cliff and Jackie went 'out' for about a year. Something that Jet found very odd suddenly came to light. Patti received a letter from Jackie. Jet was knocked sideways to discover that Cliff hadn't laid a finger on her for almost a year. Jackie was gorgeous and later went on to become Mrs. Adam Faith. Jet to this day cannot understand why they never consummated their relationship and it remained a complete mystery to him.

Cliff always liked to film some of the places that tours took them. This day in question was no exception. Cliff was out filming when Jet just happened to be walking arm in arm along the beach below the hotel balcony with a beautiful girl looking so 'in love'. Cliff didn't think anything of it, and just continued filming. On their return home some weeks later, they were all invited around to Cliff's house for a party. The film show began....

Jet and Patti sat holding hands when suddenly he appeared on the screen looking rather more than interested. Patti looked at him waiting for an explanation. Jet looked at Cliff. Cliff looked at Jet and rather hesitantly said, that he had set it up for a dare - just for fun!

Patti didn't seem overly amused. She didn't look as if she believed a word of it. Jet couldn't really blame her, for its not every day that you see your boyfriend walking along Bikini Beach in such illustrious company Jet recalled 'She was a cracker, she only had one fault, she reeked of garlic!"

Bruce for all his oddities always remained the sensible one amongst them. Jet found him asleep one day just lying there dead to the world. Jet walked over to a bowl of fruit on the table and picked up a grape, placing it gently between the cheeks of Bruce's rather large posterior! Jet recalled that it looked just like a Danish Pastry!

Regardless of what anguish Cliff put him through, Jet was always thankful for one thing from Cliff, his life. Jet remembered that they had al been invited back to some millionaires mansion for tea and Tiffin. Most of the guests were sitting around the swimming pool. Jet who was a non-swimmer at the time was standing in the shallow end having a cigarette. He suddenly had a brainwave. Swimming? Nothing to it, and off he set. He forgot about the fag! Within no time he was out of his depth and going under. Cliff by all accounts had noticed and didn't want to embarrass Jet. By this time all was not well. Cliff realised he was in trouble. He was drowning. Cliff was straight in. Needless to say, Jet learned to swim!

During the visit to South Africa, they were all invited to visit a Zulu village. Most South Africans know them as a kraal. Jet recalled that the big black chief was covered in head to foot in feathers. He sat surrounded by his spears and his eight or nine wives. One of his many daughters had taken a shine to Cliff and the chief being a kind hearted chap, offered her hand in marriage.

Before you could look round, the tribal wedding preparations had began. Jet recalled that everyone was in hysterics! Cliff looked a little embarrassed by it all. To keep the peace he went through the motions. The ceremony included having to jump hand in hand over a fire, whilst the chief muttered some strange noises. Jet said that this at last dispels the rumours. Cliff is actually married to a Zulu!

Cliff's third film, The Young Ones was in the pipeline. Jet remembered that it had been talked about for some time, but up until then hadn't been given a title. The film was eventually shot in July and featured Robert Morley and Carole Gray. Once again it was the endless early morning calls for Jet and the rest of the cast. Jet had been told that he too might be called upon to do a little acting but this never came off.

Jet was suddenly becoming bored. Before he knew it, he was heavily into drinking once again. Tony too was beginning to get restless. Nonchalance had started to creep in. They would sometimes stay a little longer in bed than the others, Jet recalled that they both liked their beds...for sleep, he added!

Jet found himself back in the studio on the 23rd May to record the main tracks for the film. The Shadows contributions to the film were, The Savage and Peace pipe. Recording sessions continued till August.

Jet along with Norrie Paramour attended the wedding of Cliff's little sister, Donna at Waltham Abbey in Essex. Jet had always had a soft spot for her...and she too knew that she was his favourite.

Six weeks at the Blackpool Opera House commencing August 28th was the start of a short season. Within two weeks, Bruce was taken ill with enteritis which had in fact affected many of the others stars who were appearing in Blackpool. Lonnie Donegan's guitarist, Les Bennett took over for a night, on September 9th. Bruce felt he was able to resume the following night, the 10th for the usual appearance at the NME all star concert at the Wembley Pool.

September the 17th found Jet at the Royal Albert Hall along with the late Adam Faith, Helen Shapiro and the John Barry Seven.

During the season at Blackpool, Jet shared a bungalow with Cliff. Jet recalled that all was now well between them and they were both looking forward to the release of the new film. It was a time for Jet to reconcile. He and Cliff would talk about anything and everything. Jet summed up Cliff's character simply by the pleasure that he had derived from The Shadows hit of Apache.

The Australian tour taking in the Far East got underway on October 14th. Jet recalled that all was well until they reached Singapore. Due to bad weather the plane made two unsuccessful attempts at landing. Jet remembered what a relief it was when they eventually landed! The two gigs in Singapore and Kuala Lumpur went well and within hours they were on their way to Australia.

The tour was to last about five weeks, taking in Sydney, Melbourne, Adelaide, Brisbane and Perth. The trip to New Zealand took in Christchurch, Auckland, Wellington and Dunedin. The overall tour was to last 35 days. During Jet's time in Australia he took up with a couple of sisters, who for unknown reason were happy to share him! Jet recalled "they used to ply him with Ouzo and the more he put down his neck the prettier they became!" It got so bad that on one occasion he didn't have a clue which sister was in bed with him. "It was never a threesome - mind you that might have been interesting!"

The liquor on those occasions seemed to flow quite freely. The sisters would always keep him supplied with plenty of water or a cup of tea to keep him revived but then he said, "It would start all over again".

Bernard Delfont supplied the road crew for the tour. Local guys were used when necessary, but E.M.I had taken care of most of the arrangements. To Jet it seemed like a life of O'Reilly. He had sun, sand, and a woman as and when he needed one.

Hank now lives in Perth with his new wife Carol. He became a Jehovah's Witness in 1973.

The flying seemed to go on forever. During one of the stopover's Jet made love to a 'real' woman. He recalls that she had 'voluptuous breasts' and was aged around forty. He was still by her age a 'babe in arms' at twenty three." We just fell into bed" Jet says that she taught him everything he needed to know and more! They met in a restaurant... and he paid!

During the trip to Singapore, Jet and one of the boys happened to be walking around the city, as ever eyeing up the local 'talent'. They had been getting quite a few encouraging looks and felt sure that they would 'score' only to discover later that they were all fellas! Singapore was, according to Jet, ripe with female impersonators especially around Boogie Alley!

Jet remembered one old dear who used to stand and scream at an office block in the middle of the town. He said that the locals would say that you could set your watch by her. She was there every day at midday screaming," You bastards, you bastards" Apparently her son used to work for the construction company involved with the building of it. When completed, he apparently fell to his death from the top of it. She blamed the building!

November the 20th found them back in Britain and things were about to change. Tony, Jet recalled, hadn't really been himself for sometime. Things seemed as if they were about to come to a head. The sessions at Abbey Road continued and all although strained seemed to be going well. December was just around the corner.

Sam Curtis one of the back-room boys had taken 'flack' from the group at one time or another, especially from Tony. Jet recalled that Tony seemed to have the knack of rubbing him up the wrong way. Suddenly Sam turned. He grabbed hold of Tony and gave him a walloping. It didn't seem to make much difference.

Jet felt that the whole situation had for some time been leading towards a fight. Sam just seemed to go purple.

He could only take so much. Tony wasn't the only one, Bruce, on occasions would put in his four-penny worth to. Jet used to call Bruce the 'Robot' due to a bad back spasm he'd sometimes get on stage. Perhaps this had something to do with his attitude towards Jet with regard to his drinking. The tours were getting harder, the playing was easy, it was the travelling.

Jet who could have the pick of any women was suddenly turning against them. They were beginning to piss him right off. The drink too was starting to take its revenge on Jet for all the abuse he had given it.

Jet was still with Patti. She did all she could to help Jet with his problem, but even her patience was beginning to wear thin. Suddenly, it wasn't working with her too.

Jet admitted that nobody said it was going to be easy. He, with the help of the bottle had ensured that his health was now starting to go down hill at an alarming rate. He didn't know where he was on some days and although he had always 'kidded' himself that he could handle it, it had now become a real problem.

Jet couldn't put it all down to Carol and Cliff. That was long past. It was all down to him. With beer inside him, he could fight anybody. Jet always seemed to pick on bigger blokes than him. Still using Vita Pointe on his hair gave ample opportunity for 'poofie' remarks to come his way. Bruce and Sam would always be there to 'help' him out of any awkward situations when he flew in a rage.

Jet said that Bruce always seemed to be the one on to him the most. He would always take it personally. Jet realised that Bruce was only doing what was right and good for him. They were heading for the top but still Jet's attitude seemed to be...'so what'. He didn't seem to give a toss.

Jet remembered working at the famous Liverpool Cavern. The Shadows walk had by now become quite famous. By the time they took the stage, Jet was well and truly gone! Bruce and Hank led the routine and Jet would follow. To his horror instead of walking back with the rest of the boys, he walked forward...straight off the stage! Jimmy Sloane who later was to work with Jet helped him back up onto the stage. The embarrassment was awful. He was saved from any serious injury by the height of the stage. He didn't fall too far! He felt the 'venom' of Bruce's anger a little later and was told to cut down on the drink in no uncertain terms!

Sam too had had to put up with Jet's drinking. Jet remembered that Sam always seemed to handle it well. Tony arrived late one night for a gig and just sat up there behind his drums. He didn't seem to care. Although Jet had his own battles to fight, he, like the rest of the group, was beginning to get a little weary of the situation. His patience to was beginning to wear thin. An argument ensued in the dressing rooms after. Tony walked out. The Shadows were without a drummer.

It didn't take long to find a replacement.

Brian Bennett joined the Shadows on October the 6th. Brian had been drumming with the Krew Kats and had been well known around Soho and seemed like the ideal replacement for Tony. Jet and Brian were to become good friends during the time that Jet was to remain with group. He like Jet enjoyed the 'odd 'pint or two. Brian assumed the mantel of looking after Jet, helping him all he could with his 'addiction' to the bottle.

Bruce initially asked Brian if he would like to join them, and to this day is still referred to as the 'new boy' even though he has remained a Shadow for some thirty years! Brian was born on the 9th February 1940, beginnng his career in music like many others in skiffle. He lists his very first instrument as washboard! He progressed to real drums with Vince Taylor as one of the Playboys in 1956/57. Marty Wilde took his services during 1958/60 becoming one of the Wildcats.

March the 11th 1962 saw Jet take the stage before Princess Margaret and the Earl of Snowden. Eton College Youth Club, Hackney Wick was the venue. Mike Berry and the Outlaws supported the show. Jet recalled that is was quite normal to perform for the aristocracy during those heady days. They would do their fair share of the Debs coming out balls.

Everybody wanted to be associated with Cliff and the Shadows. Jet remembered doing one such gig where the venue was a huge marquee on the back lawn of some Lord or Lady. It even had a chandelier hanging inside it! Parque flooring had been laid over the ground. Jet remembered that the young lady emerged with her father at the entrance to the tent, complete with a bloody great long red carpet. She turned and said,

"Oh daddy, the orchestra have arrived!"

According to Jet, there was always one who would 'fancy' you; in fact there was always one who would fancy anything in trousers! The Shadows had a name for one of the more regular 'attendees' of such functions The Sheepdog! She always seemed to be there. Her hair hung over her face like a Dulux dog! Jet remembered that you couldn't tell for sure if she was looking at you or not!

Cliff's fourth film was under review. Summer Holiday was to be filmed on location possibly in Greece. A few weeks in the sun, just what Jet was looking for. It wasn't to be... He was about to 'leave' the Shadows.

Jet's drinking had become too much for the others to bear. It couldn't go on for much longer. Bruce along with Brian had tried their best to control Jet's self-destruction course that he was heading rapidly towards.

Jet recalled that Bruce always made them all feel nervous. Sometimes before the bigger shows, Bruce would be made up and ready to go at three o'clock in the afternoon some three hours before the evening matinee! For Jet it was just another excuse to go down the pub for a pint and a game of darts!

Jet rated Bruce as a true professional. But he could on occasions take it just a little too far. Bruce was obsessed with tuning the instruments. An hour was nothing to Bruce. They had to be exactly right. He was and still is a perfectionist.

Perhaps that's what made the Shadows so good.

Tony had gone for the safety of a home life, and had fancied the idea of producing more than touring. For Jet there was never enough time in the day. Friction was beginning to creep in. Jet had been given the task as 'leader' and official spokesman for the group, and even that now was becoming unworkable.

Bruce made no secret that he didn't agree with Jet's drinking, Jet describing his own personal favourite to Bruce as a pint of shandy! Bruce knew differently, the whiskey was now ahead of a pint. Whiskey would always settle his nerves. A bottle a day was easy.

The end, when it came, was inevitable.

Jet's final appearance with the Shadows was on April 15th 1962 at the by now obligatory appearance at the NME at Wembley. Among those on the bill were Adam Faith, Helen Shapiro and Billy Fury. Jet remembered that Brenda Lee and Johnny Burnette presented the awards.

Behind the scenes the rows had began to get worse. Hank and Bruce had talked at length about it, and offered to take three months off to help Jet 'dry' out. Jet admitted that like a prat, refused as he thought he hadn't got a problem. His days had become numbered.

Jet remembered that when Brian had first joined them, he too was warned about his love of the bottle. He remembered taking Brian back-stage asking him to keep an eye out for Bruce who would watch him like a hawk. Jet would manage to hide a small bottle on his person without Bruce knowing.

The NME concert over the artistes 'green room' was to be the scene for the final scenario. Jet was informed that his services were no longer required. His first reaction was to say...

"Well, I was thinking of leaving anyway, so sod you!"
After that final performance he broke down in tears.

Brian 'Liquorice' Locking was quickly installed as Jet's replacement. Brian like Brian Bennett had played in the Krew Kats and fitted the bill perfectly. Jet said he was a very likeable man and still is to this day. Jet sat back and wished him every success.

Wonderful Land hit the top of the charts.

The severity of what had just happened didn't really sink in until much later. They were winners, but he was the loser. Patti was still there but only just, Jet being determined to make amends stating that the rest would do him good.

Jet now had time to think. It had all happened so quickly. He still needed a drink, but this time he stayed behind closed doors. He had time to reflect. The Scandinavian tour the year before had had its moments. He remembered one of the young dancers having the 'hots' for him. He himself admitted to quite fancying her even though he was with Patti. They would meet up after the show for a bite to eat, mainly just to unwind.

Jet tried relentlessly to smuggle her back to his hotel room only to be confronted by the manager. On many occasions he thought he'd cracked it only to hear the telephone ring in his room. It always seemed to be the manager.

"Mr. Harris, now you know that we do not allow that sort of thing in this hotel! Please escort the young lady from the premises!"

Jet admitted that they never ever got it together!

During one of the European stints, Hank thought he had cracked it with this German girl. Jet recalled that little did he know that they were all working girls! He remembered that the girls would seem to get friendly with you, invariably ending up with you buying the drinks. They never used to drink all of these, sometimes secretly disposing of them behind your back and on occasions pouring them onto the carpet! The more sober they were the more the punter would spend. This pleased the management of the club who didn't seem to mind the damage to the carpets as long as they kept drinking! He would replace the carpet as and when was necessary.

It was a time for remembering. Jet recalled seeing his first whale in Bergen. It was still on the boat. The smell was pretty bad so bad in fact that he promptly threw up! The show that night was just like the good old days. The cigarette lady dressed in a short black skirt and tights carrying a tray.

Bruce had taken a fancy to her so Jet recalled, but she didn't really fancy Bruce she was after him! Jet arranged to meet her the next day. Imagine his surprise when she turned up with two kids, all her bags packed, wanting to fly back to England!

Probably the most notorious incident took place in Stoke-On-Trent. Jet said that Hank and Tony were sharing a room near the theatre. All shows of the day had their usual collection of souvenir sellers, who would stand on street corners hawking pictures and the like. They weren't earning loads of money, but always seemed to be able to afford the same rooms. Jet remembered that Dave was such a guy. He used to get on well with the boys and they all knew him as a friend.

On this particular occasion Dave happened to be sharing. He, like Jet enjoyed his beer. The show had finished and Hank and Tony were sharing the double bed whilst Dave was in the single. About one o'clock they heard the door go. That must be Dave they thought. They were right it was Dave and he was well and truly legless!

Beside his bed was a sink.

Dave was making a little noise to say the least and had decided to get undressed by lying on the floor. The room began to spin. Dave was heard to say...

"Oh Jesus"

The curtains were still open and the room was fairly well lit by a light outside. Without warning Dave made a beeline for the sink...leaping over the double bed! Having had too much to drink the inevitable happened. He was sick. For a short while he seemed to regain some of his composure, Hank and Tony thinking that the worst was over – how wrong they were It started again. This time the consequences were dire! Once more he flew across the room only this time the offending stuff came from a different end! It went everywhere even on to Hank's glasses! It was awful! But still it wasn't quite over. On reaching the sink, Dave set his backside upon it.... and the sink came away from the wall!

Hank and Tony had had enough. They were up and away, after tidying themselves up as best they could, they headed back towards the theatre, managing to get in through a side door spending the rest of the night on a couple of benches!

Jet said that according to Dave the following morning the room looked as though a bomb had hit it. The manager coming in with his usual tea for three hit the roof. Dave hastily made his exit!

The 'official' photograph sellers used to follow them everywhere. They were the ones who made the money.

Jet remembered their old roadie, Sam Curtis getting in on the act. He came in to the dressing room one day during the panto season with a holdall full of half-crown pieces (12.5p) asking Jet to carry it for him. Jet remembered that it was so full he couldn't lift it! By the end of the tour Sam had bought himself a new car from the takings!

Whenever the Shadows appeared in Birmingham, they were always sure to have a good time. The girls who flocked in to see us would throw anything on to the stage. The stage was always covered with 'gifts' for Cliff. Jet recalled that one young girl had cut a long auburn plait from her hair during the show and threw it towards Cliff. The Hippodrome in Birmingham was at that time one of the only theatres without a front curtain. Jet and the rest of the group were introduced individually. Cliff would stay at a different hotel to them, which meant a better than even chance of lying in the following morning!

In those early days, Cliff's mum and dad would sometimes attend the shows, often to be seen standing in the wings. During one show at Dudley, one of the comedians, Daly and Wayne, who were appearing on the same bill asked Cliff if he would be Godfather to his newly born son, Terry. Wayne hadn't had time to arrange a christening, and suggested that perhaps on their next visit it could be arranged. Cliff duly obliged.

The days of touring for Jet were now over for the time being. When he did tour things didn't always go according to the book. He remembered that during one of the long rides up to Blackpool, they all stopped off for a cup of coffee at a cafe just outside Shrewsbury. Tony, who was fast asleep, was left in the warmth of the coach. Bruce had finished his tea before the rest and had decided to step out for some fresh air. For some reason they had forgot about Tony. Bruce hadn't and decided to check him out. The gush of warm air that hit him told him that Tony wasn't too well. The heat had sent him unconscious. Bruce dragged him out as the rest of the group emerged from the café. Jet remembered that Tony wasn't moving and his face was ashen. Eventually, they managed to revive him and after a refreshing cup of tea continued on their journey.

Not all the tricks were played by the Shadows. Cliff used to chip in every now and then with pranks of his own. Jet recalled 'repaying' his kindness to Cliff after Cliff had set him up prior to a trip to Blackpool. Cardiff had been the previous nights venue and Jet had ordered a nine o'clock call with a cup of tea for good measure. Imagine his surprise on being woken up at five o'clock in the morning! The porter didn't look too pleased according to Jet at being woken himself at that time in the morning, Jet insisting that there must be some mistake. The porter reassured him that there wasn't, the board read five o'clock, no tea! The porter went on to say that he couldn't understand why that was so early as Mr Richard wasn't getting up till ten! Jet quickly dressed and went downstairs to check the board. It had been altered. It was Cliff's handwriting!

Revenge for Jet was to be sweet! He had told Tony of Cliff's little escapade and on finding out which room he was sleeping in, decided to enter without fear. Jet remembered pulling back the covers and he and Tony emptying anything and everything into the bed! A sandwich of talc, aftershave you name it- in it went. Finally Jet and Tony tied Cliff's pink pyjamas in knots and left!

The next morning, not a word left Cliff's lips!

Jet recalled one time when Hank was asleep. He was safely dead to the world on his lilo in the gangway of a coach. For Bruce, the temptation was too great. He removed the air stopper from the bed and hysterical laughter ensued as Hank sank and hit the floor with a gentle thud!

During one of the tours Tony fell sound asleep. Jet recalled that he was always a heavy sleeper. Cliff decided to cover his face with red lipstick! Tony didn't feel a thing. On arriving at the venue, they unloaded the gear with Tony still not cottoning on. When he eventually caught sight of himself in the mirror, the air went blue!

But for the moment those days were over. Jet's services were no longer required and he began to take his enforced rest. The three years he had just gone through had soaked him with success. It was going to be difficult not being part of it. Jet wanted to taste success again.

He didn't have to wait long...it was just around the corner..

Jet, Little Richard, Gene Vincent and Sam Cooke

DIAMONDS AREN'T FOREVER.

The next few months were going to seem like an eternity. Coming to terms with what had happened wasn't going to be easy. Jet, although he didn't know it, needed the space to try and piece together his life, a life that had suddenly been turned upside down. His new live-in girlfriend, Billie Davies was to see to that. She new that rest was vital and without it he would end up drinking and worrying himself to death.

A few weeks before the split with the Shadows, his drinking had been getting steadily worse. He had met Billie sometime before on one of the tours, and as always had fallen in love with her at first sight. Billy and Jet had developed a friendship and he was besotted by her beautiful eyes. They were to become an item.

Billie was a beautiful young lady. She was to taste success with her hit record Tell Him (Decca F11572) in February 1963 ,taking it to number ten. Unlike Jet who had all ready achieved so much, Billie had been knocking on the door for some time and her follow up single in May, He's The One (Decca F11658) only reached number forty. Billie's only other noted recording; I Want You To Be My Baby (Decca F12823) gave her a brief stay at number thirty-three, in October 1968.

Billie insisted that Jet had to rest. He never answered the phone. The trauma of the few months previous, had really taken its toll. Billie was still working doing the odd tour. Jet stayed at home and followed her progress via television and radio.

Home life for Jet, something until that time had never taken preference, began to take on a whole new meaning. Things seemed to be going well, the rest was doing him good and his drinking was under control. One day the phone rang. Billie answered. It was Jack Good from Decca. Billie said it sounded important.

Jack knew that Jet had to take time off, and had the good sense not to bother him, but he needed to discuss the possibility of his return to the fray. Jet recalled that Jack asked him if he fancied going solo. A solo bass player? The thought had never crossed his mind. It couldn't work could it ?

After a discussion with Billie, Jet decided to pop in and see Jack. Jet thought that Jack must have something up his sleeve, and anyway, he had nothing to lose. The split from the Shadows had seemed like an eternity even though it had only been six weeks!

Jet accepted Jack's offer and Besame Mucho (Decca F11466) was recorded in April and released mid May 1962.Compared with the hits of the Shadows, for him it seemed only a mine success reaching number twenty-two, staying only for seven weeks. His follow up single, Main Title Theme From The Man With The Golden Arm (Decca F11488) Climbed to number twelve in August that year.

Jet and Tony hadn't really spoken to each other since the split. Tony was still quite content to sit on the sidelines. Jet on the other hand had had his imagination rekindled by the release of his two singles. Tony would have been quite content to sit back and produce. He didn't need to take to the road again. Jet recalled that he was never an up front drummer. Touring definitely wasn't one of their strongest points. It seemed to drain so much out of them. Jet had to cope with the alcohol, which had already drained him mentally and physically.

Tony had sat in on some session work, helping out John Leyton, Frank Ifield and Billy Fury. He knew that Jet was on the verge of touring again doing the odd guest spot here and there. On a visit to Scotland Jet plucked up the courage to give him a call. Although they had had some contact, the call to Tony wasn't unexpected.

Jack Good had got this idea into his head that maybe He and Tony could get together as a duo. Jet suggested that they meet up and at least give it a try, for they had nothing to lose. On Jet's return to London they met up and headed off to the studio.

Their first session involved work on 'Just For Fun', but Jack was more interested in his original idea. He always seemed to know instinctively when something was right. Jerry Lordan, an old mate form their 'Shadow' days, had come up with a couple of tunes. They sat and listened. They knew that they were onto a winner. Jack's judgement was yet again bang on target. Jet and Tony's Diamonds (Decca F11563) was to become pop history. It was the only record to hit the top of the charts featuring Drums and Bass.

Jet too had made another transition. He had switched from his original Fender to another Fender, a six string Jaguar. It was pretty unique in those days and suddenly, through Jet, it was about to catch on.

Diamonds was released in January 1963. As a twosome they had been out of the spotlight for nearly nine months. Within three weeks of its release they were back at number one. It was to stay on the chart for thirteen weeks. Much against Tony's wishes they were suddenly back on the road. The follow up single another tune from Jerry, Scarlet O'Hara (Decca F11644), was released in April and climbed to number two. Like Diamonds it too stayed in the chart for thirteen weeks. Their third and final single release Applejack (Decca F11710) made number four in September of that year.

To Jet and Tony it seemed a far cry from the days of the Shadows when the money was split four ways. They began to earn overnight. Jet was suddenly back in demand. Billie did her utmost to keep his feet well and truly on the ground. She had just released her own single and was working in her own right. Money suddenly became no object – it was easy come easy go.

Jet admitted that if it hadn't been for Billie he could have never faced the public again. She really gave him the confidence to go for it. Billie always tried to ensure that Jet stayed in a reasonable state of good health, although Jet began to kid himself that he only liked a drink, and that he had it totally under control.

People always thought the split from the Shadows was pre-planned. It always appeared that way but it wasn't. Jet and Tony never had any idea as to what they would both eventually achieve, Jet said "It just happened" Friction had been creeping in as it would when four young men are thrown together. Being one of the Shadows was like being in a pressure cooker. Jet recalled that when Diamonds was released, Bruce was green with envy. He had hoped to record Diamonds, and naturally, because of Apache, he assumed that Jerry would offer it to them. This apparent 'misplaced' loyalty from Jerry towards Bruce, led to Bruce not speaking to him for some twelve years! Jet believed that Bruce wasn't overly happy as to their success with the tune. Jet says", to be fair to Bruce, he didn't really need the money, he was well on the way to becoming a millionaire". The Shadows were still making hit records" The success of Jet and Tony had proved that there was room at the top for other instrumentalists. The only other group to have any sort of success apart from them was The Ventures who's "Walk Don't Run"

(Top Rank JAR417) had been released earlier in September 1960, climbing to number eight. Their second single Perfidies (London HLG9232) climbed to number four in December 1961.

Jet and Tony were on the crest of a wave. The year of 1963 proved to be the best year of their lives. They had come on in leaps and bounds and were voted number one instrumental group ahead of the Shadows. It couldn't last, something had to go wrong, and it did...

Jet and Billie had attended a presentation ceremony at the Savoy Hotel. Jet and Tony were gigging the following night in Worcester. After the ceremony, Jet and Billie decided to travel up overnight and jumped into their chauffeur driven car. They sped off into the night. Sleep seemed the order of the day and they both settled down on the back seat to get some rest. After about two and half hours on the road and on the outskirts of Worcester, their Humber car was in collision with a Midland Red Bus. The car was a write-off. Luckily for all three of them no one was killed.

Jet and Billie both received nasty injuries. Jet was asleep on Billy's lap and the force of the impact was so great that he lurched forward. Jet hit his head on the ashtray between the seats which split his head open from back to front. Billie also went forward hitting Jet's head and breaking her jaw. After their release from the vehicle all three were taken to the local hospital for treatment. The chauffeur received severe bruising to his legs and chest.

After an overnight stay and further examinations all three were allowed to convalesce at home. The gig that night was cancelled and after a phone call to Tony to assure them that they were both all right, they returned to their flat in Brighton. Jet and Tony were due for an appearance on Ready Steady Go that week. Jet had had half his head shaved, and couldn't face it. He, like Billie was still in severe shock. Tony still went on and did the show. Jet recalled that it was really strange that week watching Tony on TV. He could hear his guitar playing in the background but he wasn't there!

All the dates that were in the book were all cancelled as touring for Jet for the next few months was totally out of the question. He was unable to perform. The accident had taken him out of the spotlight. Suddenly the fame was gone. He locked himself away; unable to record he became a recluse.

Billie and Jet were both compensated for the accident and Jet believes that he never truly recovered after that knock to his head. Call it fate, perhaps that's the way it was meant to be.

Jet and Tony never recorded again.

The months that followed were to be a healing process as Jet and Billie nursed each other back to health. Because of Billie's broken jaw (her mouth had been wired up) there was always a set of wire cutters just in case she began to vomit. Jet remembered that it couldn't have been much fun drinking through a straw! The knock to his head did him no favours. He was to suffer bouts of amnesia and began drinking like there was no tomorrow. For Jet there was nothing else to do and it became just another excuse.

Alcoholism is just one excuse after another and he could always find an excuse for a drink.

On good days funny stories would come to mind. Jet remembered without mentioning any names, a rather funny incident happening whilst he was with the Shadows appearing at Blackpool. He was relaxing in the dressing room whilst another member of the group was actively' engaged' with a young lady. Having seen it on numerous occasions he took no notice. As a group they had all been there one time or another. Judging by the look on her face, she was enjoying it too! That look was about to change...

Suddenly a reporter complete with camera from the Melody Maker burst into the room to conduct an interview. The guy in question looked up and on the spur of the moment said *"You haven't met the fan club secretary have you?"*

Well the rest just fell about laughing and Jet recalled that they didn't even get a picture! Jet and Billie had their funny moments too.

Billie was fast sleep one morning and Jet who had always been one for practical jokes decided that morning was to be no exception. If the opportunity arose he would take it. He couldn't resist what happened next. Gently pulling back the sheets he revealed Billie's backside. He drew a face on the cheeks of her backside in indelible ink! Well much to his surprise, she didn't notice it, even when taking a bath. No one ever really looks at their backside now do they? Jet recalled that it seemed to go on for weeks. One day she got out of the bath and he just stood there laughing. She suddenly saw it and went ape-shit, calling him all the names under the sun!

Billie often put herself in the firing line. Jet remembered that they were touring one day along with Tony. She wanted to go to the toilet. There was no toilet aboard the bus so the coach driver stopped and Billie headed off for the nearest clump of bushes. There was a bit of a scream. She had sat on some stinging nettles! Everyone including Billie saw the funny side of it!

There had been many tours during the last three years. This one featured Gene Vincent, Little Richard and Sam Cooke. Gene had always been one of Jet's idols so to tour with him was something special. Sadly like Sam, Gene is no longer with us. His career spanned some five years with Pistol Packin'Mamma (Capitol CL15136) getting to number fifteen back in June 1960. His most famous one "Be Bop A Lula" (Capitol CL14599) climbing to number sixteen in August 1956. Jet always got on with Gene. He was one of the old rockers and Jet missed him sadly.

Jet also remembered the legendary Sam Cooke. Not only was Sam a gentleman but he was also a gentle man.

He like Gene was one of the early influences in the 50's having tasted success with Only Sixteen (HMVPOP642) number twenty three, in August 1959, and later from September 1960-March 1962 attaining three records in the top ten, Chain Gang (RCA1202) number nine, Cupid (RCA 1242) number seven and Twisting The Night Away (RCA1277) reaching number six in March 1962.Sam's highest entry was Wonderful World (RCAPB49871) which was a re-issued single in 1986 after its previous shot had only climbed to number twenty seven in July 1960. Jet said that compared to Little Richard he was a saint!

Little Richard had been on the scene since December 1956.He had five top ten entries with Long Tall Sally (London HLO8866) number three, February 57. The Girl Can't Help It (London HLO8882) number nine, March 57. Lucille (London HLO8446) number ten, June 57,Good Golly Miss Molly (London HLU8560) number eight, February 58 and his highest with Baby Face (London HLU8770) reaching number two in January 1959.

Jet had always admired Little Richard. "He was pure energy - he was just phenomenal!"

Billie and Jet were to remain together for about eighteen months. The accident was to keep Jet out of work for nearly three years. He still kept in touch with Winnie and Bill quite regularly, feeling that his was the period in his life when he needed them the most if only to be there. He felt close but sadly he was drifting further and further away from them. Like all parents, they were still very concerned for their son and especially for his welfare. But it was down to him. He and only he had the solution to his problems.

Work had suddenly become non-existent, and with none on the horizon, he began to find his friends again... at the bar. Billie stuck with him through thick and thin, trying desperately to understand his needs. She decided to contact a Harley Street Specialist. His subsequent visit ended up with an injection of ECT, which Jet said wasn't the standard procedure for alcoholism. The specialist informed him that he had a small 'shadow' on his brain. It was to give him cause for concern for some time to come.

Jet and Billie seemed to become closer. He asked her to marry him and Billie accepted yet Jet's fight against alcoholism put a stop to that marriage. He didn't help himself. It was down to stubbornness' wanted desperately to get better. So did Billie. There was nothing she could do...from being close...they began to lose their way.

Jet and Billie shared two flats, one in Brighton and one in Chelsea. They left Brighton and returned to London. His career in music was over. Tony had returned to producing. By this time Jet had nothing but memories.

Within weeks Billie moved out. For the first time in his life he was alone. He shut himself away whilst still trying to fight the bottle which was proving difficult. By now, the bottle had governed even his eating habits. He began to eat less and drink more. He wanted a woman in his life and felt that he had come full circle. For the last seven years he had enjoyed fast cars, travel and many women. His money was beginning to run out. He had started with nothing, and looked like he was about to end up with nothing.

Jet had to take on the role of a single man. He just had to survive. His next- door neighbour in Chelsea was the infamous Viv Prince from The Pretty Things. Jet wasn't into their sort of music, but at least they were on the scene. Out of Vic's seven releases with the band between June 1964 and August 1966, only Don't Bring Me Down (Fontana TF503) made the top ten, peaking at number ten. Jet remembered that they were a cult band with Viv often living up to his reputation by doing odd things like bringing Jet bacon and eggs at four in the morning reeking of garlic!

Jet's daily ritual of hauling himself off the pillow to be greeted with empty bottles was fast becoming a blur. He was somewhat blind to the fact that he had become a drunkard. He had had the fame and like Viv he too was becoming infamous with his reputation for drinking.

The truth was that no one wanted to know Jet Harris.

On one of the days he ventured out he ended up in the bar just around the corner from his flat. He just sat there minding his own business when he was approached by a young lady who had just come in with her mum and dad.

"Your Jet Harris aren't you?"

He smiled and said" Yes I am"

He went over to their table and joined them. Jet remembered that she too had the same surname as him her name...Anita Harris. They sat talking for a while totally unaware of his own personal problems. She told Jet that she would become famous one day and she did! Jet had noticed the young lady working behind the bar on numerous occasions. She had seen him, but for some unknown reason hadn't recognised him. On hearing his name she came over to their table.

"Is that right your Jet Harris?"

"Yes" he replied.

"Well you're not going to believe this, but my mother stitched your head for you a couple of years back."

What a small world thought Jet. They were to get on quite famously! Anita's mum and dad had every confidence in their daughter's quest for success. Just Loving You (CBS2724) gave her a top ten hit in June 1967,reaching number six and staying n the charts for some thirty weeks.

Looking back over the years, Jet had been involved in quite a few accidents. He was with Carol and Hank one time when their car burst into flames! Carol, who was pregnant with Ricky, managed to get out of the car. She landed in the street. Jet was still driving in a state of stunned silence. In a panic he hit a wall, breaking his collarbone and bruising his ribs. Hank suffered a pair of broken glasses!

Jet admitted to having had a couple of beers prior to getting into the car. Unlike today, the law regarding drink/driving didn't apply. He got away with it. Jet must have been mad for he returned to the car to switch off the engine...while it was still on fire!

Carol who by this time was quite hysterical was crying "My baby, my baby!" The people who had happened to witness the whole thing believed that there was a baby on board and were most concerned when they couldn't find it!

It was always Jet who ended up in these scrapes. During his time with the Shadows he would frequent a lot of bars. He would think nothing of 'jetting' off across London to pay off money that he owed to obliging Landlords. Hank again was in the car. Every pub Jet entered to pay, he would have one for the road. Inevitably six or seven pubs down the road it had got to his legs! He smashed the car into an oncoming vehicle. Again, luckily, no one was hurt.... except Hank... He managed to break his glasses!

Jet thinks that he used to have a death wish with his specs! They were all that seemed to get damaged!

Sue Speed turned out to be the barmaid's name. They seemed to hit it off right away. Well they had something in common. Jet wanted to see more of her and she of him. It became a regular occurrence. Jet the ever hopeful had again 'fallen in love' and believed that she was just what he was looking for.

He never had eyes for anyone else.

As their relationship blossomed, she learned of his fight against drink. She felt like all the others that she could help. Being Jet Harris helped when it came to romance. Jet always let his heart rule his head. Within weeks Sue wanted more out of this relationship, she wanted it to be permanent. He wasn't too sure at first, but after considering all things she eventually moved in. Sue missed her parents and Jet seemed to get the impression that she would like to return to her roots.

Sue had originated from Evesham. Jet remembered the look on her mum and dads face when he walked in to ask for their daughter's hand in marriage! Sue's mum had never like the idea of her daughter working in the city, and deep down hoped that one day she would return. She decided to apply for a position working at a local hotel. Application accepted Jet and Sue moved to Cheltenham.

Within weeks they were married.

Jet and Sue rented a flat in Cheltenham. He stayed home. She went to work. Jet's income was only coming from royalties from his previous recordings. He soon began to carve a new niche. While Sue was working, he was back to drinking. With nothing to do in the daytime the local pubs became his second home. For Sue, being married to Jet Harris was to prove very difficult. She tried to cope with his problem to the best of her ability.

Within six months they were to part. Sue couldn't cope She couldn't face the thought of coming home to find Jet in a drunken state night after night. Blazing rows seemed the norm. It just wasn't working. The marriage was annulled.

Jet and Sue never really got it together. Their life styles were so different. The only thing that they had in common was drink. She used to serve it at the hotel - he would drink it at any pub. They did however work together at a local pub in Cheltenham. The Tankard and Castle (Goat and Bicycle) in Hesters Way. This seemed to work for a while as Sue could keep an eye on him full time!

During the first few months of their brief but stormy relationship, they seemed besotted with each other. Being in the vicinity of drink, isn't the best therapy for someone with a problem and Jet recalled it was like a red rag to a bull. According to Jet, working with drink never seemed to bother him. It was readily available, but he drank less! He remembered staying quite sober; anyway he couldn't be seen to be drunk behind the bar!

Jet's musical career had been on hold for what seemed an eternity. He had been invited to London to discuss the resurrection of his career. He dropped Sue off at the pub and journeyed on down for the meeting. Sue was having other ideas. The landlords wife had been taken into hospital and with Jet being away for a few days anything could happen...

Jet returned to the pub to find that the landlord had been having a fling with Sue. It had been going on while his wife was in hospital! Jet returned just before she was discharged. Discovering what had gone on, she threatened to commit suicide, actually throwing herself out of an upstairs window! The proverbial, according to Jet, hit the fan!

She was returned to hospital with a pair of broken legs!

For Jet that was the straw that broke the camels back. Sue disappeared whilst Jet stayed on at the pub for a few more weeks. Finally under great stress he left. He recalled that the landlord couldn't face him. He looked for his friends at the bar.

When the split with Sue became reality, Jet felt like a broken man. Looking back he admitted that she wasn't right for him. Perhaps she was a means to an end as at the time he had needed someone and she just happened to be there. He left Cheltenham and returned to London.

Jet did the odd days in the studios guesting as a session musician, but the magic had gone. Winnie and Bill had moved to Watford and with the fear of deep depression looming ever closer, he rang them and asked them if he could come home.

The homecoming wasn't an emotional affair. His lifestyle had cramped whatever contact he had with them;

He knew he should have kept in touch more often. Winnie and Bill still welcomed him warmly. They both knew that he had some sort of problem with alcohol but never to what extent. If they did know, they certainly kept it secret from Jet.

Life at home was easy with Winnie and Bill doing all they could to give him their best. For his part he made a visible effort to control his drinking, but within weeks he was again getting restless. Jet loved his mum and dad dearly, but like all parents who want the best for their children, they were beginning to irritate him He began to spend more and more time away from the house. He had no real trade apart from his music. His brief spell as a barman being all he had done, he hadn't really been interested in anything. Perhaps a career change was the answer. He needed a new challenge. Big or small, it didn't matter. He decided to look for work.

The period that followed wasn't easy. He had met up with a lady from Selsey, Anne Frascetti with whom he was to have a fleeting affair. He left home and set up house with her in Bognor Regis. Renting a small place close by, Jet applied for a vacancy as a Kennelman. The job entailed more than just feeding them, he had to train them too, to become guard dogs. Not being overly fond of dogs, the challenge seemed irresistible. He decided t have a go.

Jet recalled that the guy who ran the business was a right oddball. Like Jet, he enjoyed a drink too. When he was sober he was a really funny guy, but when he'd had a few, watch out! His pride and joy was a Lotus car. He went everywhere in it. Whenever he wasn't there Jet had to be on his guard, especially around lunchtime. He used to carry a shotgun in the car, and on his return would often jump out of his car and try and shoot you!

One day Jet noticed his car coming up the drive. He wasn't driving too straight and thought "here we go again". Out came the gun. Jet thought sod this I'm off! and with that jumped from the first floor window to the ground some ten feet below. The landing wasn't what he had bargained for...He smashed the ball of his foot quite badly. The boss for once left the gun downstairs and on hearing Jet's cries for help, phoned for an ambulance to take him to hospital.

Anne saw the funny side of it at first, but didn't like the thought of him being at home all day. She wanted to be kept but without a wage coming in, that would be nigh on impossible. Jet was to find himself on his own yet again. Anne upped and left. His foot was in plaster and he hobbled around on crutches for a couple of months.

Royalties were still coming in on a regular basis and, with money not a problem, he decided that once again he needed a change of scenery. He needed to get away. A quick skip through the holiday brochures and his mind was made up. A couple of weeks in Jersey seemed just the ticket. He packed his bags and caught the plane...

It was to be some holiday...He was to stay in Jersey for five years!

MAGGIE...

Time had raced on. It was 1971.It had been nearly nine years since his departure from the Shadows and with two broken marriages behind him and four years of nondescript existence the future didn't look too bright. He was a little apprehensive as to what it might hold.

Before his arrival in Jersey life had dealt him many blows. His drinking certainly hadn't done him any favours, most of the time just remembering the last drink. He was hoping that the two weeks in Jersey would give him the lift that he was looking for. He was going to enjoy himself regardless and of course sink a few pints!

For the locals it must have been strange to see this little man hobbling around with one leg in plaster. The comings and goings to and from the pub each day must have turned some heads. It wasn't long before he was amongst the ladies again.

One evening Jet walked into the local for his usual evening session. He was pretty 'tanked' up from the day but still pretty sober. Looking round the room he spotted a table around which a group of young ladies were sitting. Thinking nothing of it, he went over to sit by them. The ladies probably weren't very impressed by the intrusion, being out for a quiet drink, but he was determined to strike up a conversation. During the evening one of the group a pretty young Scottish lass seemed to take an interest in him. She didn't know who he was, and because his leg was in plaster, seemed to feel a little sorry for him. He introduced himself and she still didn't realise who he was.

They seemed to hit it off right away. The next time he saw her he was on the sea front and this time he was sober!

Maggie had come over to Jersey to do a nursing course, and being 'essentially employed' meant that she could remain as a resident on the island. For most people, their income governs their residency, but with Maggie she could remain without the necessary income controls. Within days they were setting up home together. Jet had decided that it looked like a good idea, and Maggie didn't seem to have any objections. Most days were spent down the pub. Maggie would work shifts and their time together was governed by her hours. His money was fast disappearing, so he decided to look for work.

Music had been his life. During his stay on the island, he made many guest appearances at local clubs and hotels.

Maggie worked at the local hospital and Jet, whose leg was now out of plaster, decided to try his hand as a porter. Not really being cut out for this, he noticed an advertisement for a second chef. During the interview the guy asked him about his experience. Jet told him that he had worked at a Bistro in Sloane Square, London. When asked to produce his references, Jet told him he couldn't because the place had accidentally burnt down! He took him on! Jet in fact didn't know the first thing about kitchen work; he just picked it up as he went.

Jobs seemed to be on offer all over the island. Living by the sea was to give him the opportunity to try his hand as a trawler-man. It was during this period that he was to experience his worst ever nightmare. Jet remembered that they were out to sea and the wind was blowing a fair gale. Curly the skipper was busy winching the nets. A gust of wind suddenly engulfed his apron and dragged it into the winch. Jet and the rest of the crew could only stand there and watch helplessly as the rope around the winch ripped part of his arm away. After a desperate struggle they managed to release him and stem the flow of blood, which was quite fierce. They radioed for help and on their return to port an ambulance was waiting to take him to hospital. Frank, Curly's son, stayed back to moor the boat as Jet went ashore to accompany him to hospital.

Jet had had many shaking fits in his life mainly due to the bottle, but this was different. He began to shake from shock. His whole body was going. He thought a pint of beer might 'steady' his nerves. No chance...he got a cup of sweet tea! Curly's arm was repaired and he eventually went back to sea.

Jet's jobs were numerous and varied to say the least. He was to try his hand as a lobster pot man, a potato picker, a roof tiler and even planting Gladioli. There seemed nothing he wouldn't try.

With his 'settlement' on the island reasonably secure thanks to Maggie, he was to make quite a few friends. An associate of his, Billy used to bring him spider crabs. Costing only two shillings (10p) Jet developed quite an appetite for them. Billy arrived one day and knocked on the door of the flat. Jet had had rather a lot to drink that day and asked Billy if he could put the crab on the floor and he would pick it up and pay him later. Jet completely forgot about it. Three days later he heard this noise coming from beneath the sofa. The bloody thing was still alive! Jet was filled with remorse and walked to the harbour returning it to the sea.

Jet and Maggie seemed reasonably happy. His drinking wasn't helping. Maggie like all those before kept at it hoping that things would improve. She even bailed him out of gaol. He had had so much he couldn't stand, so a night in the cells was the only option.

The island itself is a really beautiful place. Believe it or not, it is full of alcoholics. Money's no object out there. From Maggie's point of view, he wasn't the easiest of people to live with. They used to row a lot about his addiction and the problems that went with alcohol. There were times when Maggie thought he was beyond help. But she had become rather fond of him and always clung on to the belief that one-day he would get better. There were times when he would just wander off neither he nor she knowing where he was.

Maggie tried her utmost to keep him on the rails. He spurned all help. He abused it and thought that he knew best. Maggie had to strike where it hurt. She got him banned from five pubs on the island. He still managed to get in his quota in the numerous small bars and clubs dotted around the place. His addiction wasn't doing Maggie any favours. Her weight dropped to six stone six pounds during this period. She was sick with worry. She was above all beginning to wonder what she had let herself in for. She was beginning to lose hope. Jet was losing her.

All the days weren't the same. Life on the island was very easy going, and when the sober moments took him, Jet could be found studying the wild life. He had always had a secret love of flowers and insects, ever since he could remember. During his early days with Cliff he thought nothing of carrying a camera round taking pictures whenever he could. He had always wanted to take photos of these strange little things, and his wish was to come true some time later.

The time had flown by. Jet had been with Maggie for nearly five years! Her course at the hospital had gone as far as it could, and she decided to return to the mainland, to follow a course in midwifery at Cheltenham. Jet and Maggie had actually gone their separate ways a few weeks before, but had stayed friends having shared so much time together. They said goodbye at the airport even shaking hands.

It was 1976.

Jet was alone. He stayed on at the flat for a short while. He had made a terrible mistake. He wanted Maggie. He decided to track her down. He knew where she was working and just turned up at the hospital. He begged her for a second chance. He knew that they had found something together in Jersey.

To prove he meant business he took a job locally working on the buses! Promising her that things were going to get better Maggie took pity on him and decided to give it another go.

Maggie had only been back in England a few weeks. Jet still needed a crutch, someone to lean on. Maggie was his only lifeline apart from the bottle. The effort that he put in must have worked for within months they were married. Cheltenham hadn't seen anything quite like it. Reporters from the Sunday Express splashing their pictures all over the place.

Jet had told Maggie that being married would give him more security and the strength to fight and seek help with his problem. One problem Jet didn't foresee was Maggie's mother! On seeing the press release she was on her way down from Scotland! She was fuming. She didn't approve of the marriage, thinking that her daughter could have done better. Here she was marrying a bus conductor!

She knew of his infamous behaviour and didn't mince her words. Jet was well and truly out for the count.

Before Jet and Maggie set up home, Jet spent some time in a small hotel run by a Chinese man. It was chop suey every night! One of the worst occupations that he took up before bus conducting was at Taylors Skin yard, working with animal skins. Jet recalled 'it was awful some of these skins were still warm!' He had the urge to travel again so bus conducting it was!

Although Maggie's mother didn't approve of the marriage, she didn't actually dislike Jet. She thought of him as a loveable rogue. He was beginning to get his head back together. He had managed to secure the services of some local lads and the odd gig here and there supplemented his income. He hadn't 'lost' touch with the music business, it was as and when it happened.

Home for Jet and Maggie was a mobile caravan at Little Whitcombe near Cheltenham. A small site nicely situated and close to all the main routes in and around Gloucester. His drinking seemed to go in fits and starts. He would remain sober for days and then suddenly get stoned. Maggie wasn't going to stand for any nonsense from him.

The site had many trees. Jet remembered coming back from the pub one day deciding that he was going to build a tree house for the kids on the site. He was up in the branches when suddenly he hit the ground from some twelve feet up! Maybe the alcohol softened the blow. His backside was a little tender for a couple of weeks!

The three years that Jet and Maggie were to spend on that site were probably the best years of his life. His first son by Maggie was born. Ben was a lovely child. They had so much fun together. He felt part of a family unit, something that Jet had probably wanted all along.

Jet was to work on the buses for some ten months. He gained a bit of a reputation, passengers sometimes refusing to pay him their fares. Many days one could hear...Sod off Harris, we ain't paying you! Jet's driver was a funny sort of bloke too. Jet remembered that he had developed a thing about his girlfriend, constantly worrying about what she was up to during the day. He was driving past her house one day and noticed her naked through the glazed front door. It wasn't her naked he could see, it was her backside pressed up against the door. Jet seemed to think that she was actively engaged in some kind of 'therapy' with someone else! He told the driver not to be so stupid it was just his imagination!

They were good times. In those days the conductor would always shout out the names of the villages as the bus went through. Not Harris...He would shout out the names of the public houses!

"OK girls its the Cross Hands at Brockworth or the Bell at Shurdington"

Jet used to ring the bell, telling the passengers that he had to use the toilet. He would jump off the bus and race into the pub. The landlords knew him well. They would have a pint waiting for him on the counter! He would be in and out in about one and a half minutes, and then on to the next one! No one ever knew! The serge suits they wore did his legs no good either.

They would be red raw by the end of the day.

The machine box for the ticket machine wasn't gainfully employed! Jet would fill it with little bottles of Gold Label! He remembered the fun they had winding the destination on the front and back of the bus. The driver used to be a right card. Jet remembered that many a time he would talk to the old dears with their shopping bags and walking sticks as they tried to get on the back step of the bus. He would pretend to 'wind' the step down saying, "Is that alright for you now my love?"

Invariably they would say yes. Jet said that the stick to an old person in Cheltenham is like a badge of honour. The driver was an Irishman. Being noted for his practical jokes Jet remembered that he got his mate one day to don a pair of dark glasses and walk with a white stick. All very well you might think, but on this occasion he led him and sat him down in the drivers seat! The passengers just sat there looking totally bewildered. He said,

"You know where the gear stick is?" he said "Yes" "And you can feel the pedals?" "Yes!"

The passengers got off...The driver he lost his job!

Life on the site was pretty laid back. Jet and Maggie had a pet dog called Dougal. He used to keep Jet in check especially if he had had a few that night and happened to be taking it out on Maggie. He would often grab Jet's trouser leg spin round, and trip him over!

All the residents on the site would pull together. They were all happy. On milk days when the milkman came round for his money, most of them would lie on the floor hiding...he hardly ever got paid! Being on a caravan site gave up its fair share of mice and things. Jet found one in the caravan one day. It was as big as a rat! A quick whack with the broom and it was away.

Jet and Maggie and their new child really wanted a more permanent home. They were soon to move to a house in Gloucester. Cleveland Road was a far cry from their mobile home. For them it was a step in the right direction. Jet remembered that they were all sad to leave the site, but have remained friends with many of the residents till this day. For Jet and Maggie they were happy memories.

The new home had given them a proper bedroom and space to move about. They had a garden instead of a patch of ground. Jet's musical ventures were bringing in a few extra pennies and coupled with Maggie's income they seemed to cope quite well. Jet had improved his standing in Maggie's eyes; his drinking wasn't causing too many problems. No sooner said than done, complacency set in. Just when all seemed well, he began to drift back into his old ways. The pub was to dominate his life once again. One visit became two, two became three. He wanted it to end but he was powerless to stop it.

Maggie was now pregnant with his second son. Sam was born on the 8th March 1980. A month before the birth he had stayed sober for the sake of Maggie. Jet missed the birth. He slipped out for a quick cigarette. It would have been a first for him to witness a birth but like most expectant dads he needed a fag!

Sam's birth was more than an excuse to go for a drink. He headed for the first off licence and purchased the biggest bottle of champagne they had. That night he got legless!

The birth of Sam, had given Jet the opportunity to really make a go of it. He had responsibilities. He had a wife and two lovely children. He decided enough was enough. The drink had to go. It didn't last long. Within two months he was as bad as ever. Maggie was beginning to despair.

Maggie remembers that he came home one night drunk as usual and she was so angry that she threw a chair at him. She remembers him retaliating so violently that she received two black eyes. He threw a mega-fit. She remembers him punching at anyone and anything. Alcohol can do all sorts of things to a person. With Jet its like Jekyll and Hyde. He threw her a couple of quid and disappeared out of the door, heading off to Jersey for a couple of weeks to hit the bottle. He had totally messed up. The week away from Maggie was probably the longest he had spent apart during all their years together. He returned home full of remorse begging for forgiveness.

They were still together.

Jets involvement with music albeit locally had sparked interest elsewhere. He landed a spot on one of the 'Oh Boy!" tours along with his old girlfriend, Billie Davies. Maggie seemed quite pleased that some real money was about to come over the threshold. Maggie would support him when he wasn't working. Staying sober was the name of the game. If he wasn't sober he didn't play...if he didn't play there were no pennies!

Maggie had passed her final exams qualifying now as an S.R.N. For her it had been a long haul. Training and examinations along with Jet's tantrums were difficult enough, she had equipped herself well. Living with Jet wasn't easy. At home he would try to do his fair share of raising his two boys. They weren't exactly toddlers anymore and with Maggie doing shift work, it was down to him.

Coney Hill a hospital that specialises in all sorts of medical disorders became a much frequented place for Jet.' Drying out' had now become a regular thing. It was during his first visit he was to meet up with another woman Jackie, who, like Jet, was recovering from the effects of alcohol. Jet discovered that she had some personal problems mainly back home. They seemed to hit it off immediately. She became a good friend of the family, and unbeknown to Jet at that time, was to be a part of his life a little later.

Maggie had often threatened to leave Jet if he didn't seek help with his drink problem. She for one was pleased that her husband was at last beginning to see the light. Jet's first visit lasted three days. He came out with an 'all clear'. Three days without a drink had seemed like a lifetime to him. It seemed to have done him good. Some of the people in there were a lot worse of than him, and he had seen first sight, some of the effects that excessive amounts of liquor could do to someone's body.

The hospital also did training courses. Special therapy and work experience were all part and parcel of the 'drying out' process. During another visit he was placed on an electronics course at Fishponds, Bristol. The course was interesting, but the travelling to and from Bristol everyday was dreadful. He decided to look for a job closer to home.

A vacancy had arisen at a company who produced fruit machines based in Chalford, near Stroud. He was to meet up there with a guy called Alec Merrick who was to become his best friend and roadie during the years to come.

Jet was still travelling to work by car and despite all the efforts of the hospital he was still drinking. He would stop off most days for his cigarettes and when available a small bottle of vodka. The journey to and from work took him over the top of Slad Valley, stopping off to empty the contents of the bottle down his neck before he reached work. Jet convinced himself that it was the only way to sort out how to stop drinking. He would roll up at work quite merry but was always able to do his job.

Marianne Electronics threw up a catch phrase that both Jet and Alec use to this day. Both hard at it, Alec suddenly made a mistake and came out with 'bumhole!' Both Alec and Jet burst into fits of hysterical laughter, the phrase seeming to take over their days. It got so bad that Alec used to sing the word to well known tunes, the most noted being the theme from Snow White and the Seven Dwarfs. It was quite normal to hear the sounds of the dwarfs going off to work to the strains of Bumholeee! Alec and Jet still greet each other this day with the same expletive! It became so much a part of their lives that it even rang out when a certain member of the management came into the factory. To Alec it will best be remembered as the warm up for the Dallas Boys who in harmony, used to loosen up their vocal chords before going on stage!

Jet and Alec were to spend many happy hours together on the road. But suddenly Jet's world was to fall apart. Winnie and Bill had been there forever. Although his visits weren't as frequent, they were still there. Sadly, in January 1983,Bill passed away.

The Christmas before Jet and Maggie had invited them both over to spend Christmas with them. Bill had already been admitted to hospital after suffering a heart attack a few weeks before. Jet and Maggie thought that the ideal place to recuperate and enjoy the grandchildren would be with them. Christmas went well and all seemed fine. Bill and Winnie returned home and on January the 13th Maggie took a call from the hospital. Bill had been admitted once again after suffering a relapse. He died a little while later. Jet was devastated.

When someone who has always been there suddenly disappears, you wish you had perhaps given just a little more of your time to him or her. Looking back and leaving home at such a young age coupled together with his career didn't leave him much time. Whatever time Jet had he always seemed to be elsewhere. Winnie and Bill were always there. Old folks just seem to go on forever. The time he had just spent with them was ironically more precious than before. Jet would always have fond memories of his father, Maggie, Ben and he spent many happy hours with him at their home in Clacton. He would always remember Bill with great love. It was he who encouraged the young Harris to pursue his dreams.

Whenever times were hard, his father was always there. He was a lovely man and Jet missed him dearly.

Jet and Maggie were soon to leave Cleveland Road. They had wanted to find somewhere else for sometime. A semi-detached cottage 'Mafeking' in Elmore Lane, Quedgeley Gloucester was to be the new family home. For Jet and Maggie it was to be their best days together since the caravan at Little Whitcombe. The house was ideally situated, just off the main road with a lovely garden. Jet decided to turn his hand to photography.

He had always had a flair for photography and as the word got around he received many commissions for work. Industrial and promotional work took up most of the day, leaving very little time to pursue a full time musical career. Drink wasn't a problem. His work kept him too busy. He would think nothing of sitting all day waiting for the right moment to capture an insect or a spider on film. Life had some meaning. He was beginning to gain some respect.

Alcoholics however sober they may look to the outside world will always find the bottle again. Jet was no exception. It was all going too well. He was becoming successful in his own right and gaining a reputation for his work. He thought the odd beer wouldn't do any harm...it did. He began to hide drinks all over the place. Maggie says "He was a perfectionist"

Maggie recalls that a stay over one night at a hotel proved the point. Terry was getting drunker by the minute and she couldn't understand why. She knew he was still drinking but supposedly in moderation. She discovered that he had been hiding drinks in the rafters of the ceiling of the hotel. She literally hit the roof!

Maggie says that maybe his addiction to alcohol started when he was very young. Being fed gripe water by the bottle didn't help. After all it's about 95% alcohol! Maybe the 'drug' has been in his system since he was barely able to walk. The port and lemons he used to partake of didn't have any affect on him all those years ago, continuing to drink them until he was twelve years of age!

Jet admitted that maybe Maggie was right. Maggie said that a mutual friend of theirs once said that 'the reason an alcoholic never commits suicide is because he is afraid that he will miss the next drink'.

Life at Mafeking went with the flow. Maggie's only real time off work was to have the children. Craig, his third son was to arrive a little later. Jet had struck up an association with Norman and Maggie Brodie an agency dealing with entertainment. They lived a little further down Elmore Lane. Jet would wander over most days, mainly for the company. Norman had offered to take Jet on and had arranged a few gigs locally.

Norman had managed to get him on to a rock n roll tour and it looked like Jet was about to turn the corner. He had a lot to prove especially to himself and with that in mind Norman continued to place him locally, the tour being a bonus. Jet wanted it to happen immediately. Norman couldn't risk anything nationally until he had proved himself capable of not depending on alcohol.

Jet's impatience lead him back to drinking. Alec had teamed up with Jet, and he above any others kept Jet in check. Being Jet Harris meant that everybody wanted to pat you on the back. Everybody wanted to buy you a drink...who was he to refuse?

Despite Alec, Norman and Maggie, it was back to Coney Hill. He stayed for three weeks. Jet remembered that 'although you are not physically locked in your rooms, you were not allowed to leave the hospital.' Jackie was still making her family visits. Maggie found her quite funny. Unbeknown to Maggie Jet had already struck up a strong relationship with Jackie. It had begun to develop over the previous year. His marriage was about to hit rock bottom.

Norman and Maggie had invited them both to join them on holiday in Cornwall. The break would do them good. Maggie was sensing that all was not well. On their return it all came out. Jet admitted to Maggie that they were an item. He told her that he loved Jackie. Her reaction was no different than what he had expected. She told him to leave and if that's what he wanted then go and live with her. Maggie was seven months pregnant with Craig. Jet's insensitivity to the situation at that time was highlighted by his revelation that he had never been in love with anyone as much as Jackie. This cut Maggie deeply.

Jet admitted that if there was one thing that he and Maggie had it was the ability to communicate. They were always good talkers. Maggie told him 'that if you were in love with someone that much you would live in a tent, nothing else would take precedent'.

Jet stepped back and began to have mixed loyalties. He desperately loved his family. Maggie had come through so much and they had come together so far. Mafeking and its security were pulling. His timing once again had been impeccable. He told Maggie that he wanted to just get Jackie out of his system. He was kidding himself. Once again Maggie said if that's what you want then go and do it.

The next few months were a nightmare. He began to flit between the two. He thought he'd got it cracked. He had the best of both worlds. Suddenly he was out on his ear. Maggie had gone along with his idea of 'working her out of his system' only to be lied to. He was told to pack his bags and get out.

Jet left Mafeking on December 18th 1985.Maggie was within 23 days of the birth of her third baby. Craig Harris was born on the 10th January 1986. It was Christmas and he had just walked out on his wife and boys for another woman. The grass always looks greener on the other side. No one in the right mind would walk out on a woman who was eight and half months pregnant. Maggie had been left totally stranded. Jet regretted to this day what he did to her and the boys. He had it made. They were right for each other. He had blown it all away, like a piece of paper in the wind.

Two days or so after Craig's birth, he made out that he wanted to come back. He arrived at the hospital, drunk. He had no idea where he was. Maggie was informed that her husband was waiting to see her. She agreed to let him in. Maggie said that he was in a dreadful state.

The next few months Jet drifted in and out of their lives. It was like a game of chess with Maggie and Jackie the pawns. He never gave his boys the time of day that Christmas, he was more interested in the new love of his life. Jackie.

Jet remembered both he and Jackie once told Maggie that she was mad, and incapable of anything. Jet had seen his solicitor advising him to warn Maggie to stay away. It couldn't go on like this. The eighteen months that followed he used them both for his own ends. Jackie called Maggie everything under the sun. Jet sat back and got away with murder. He hadn't given his children any love or support. Jet admitted he was a total bastard.

Not all the times spent with Maggie were bad. Jet remembered how they both looked for houses in and around Gloucester, before settling on Mafeking. Their children's education was an obvious priority. They had both fallen in love with a property in the Forest Of Dean but it only had one problem...it was on the side of a hill. Maggie suffered from vertigo and Jet recalled her saying,

"Och Aye Terry, I canna live on the side of a hill". The house in question had a lovely garden except it was about a one in five gradient! Jet admitted that it wouldn't have been any use the pub was too far, about a mile away, and he didn't fancy walking home in the dark!

Maggie knows only too well what alcohol can do to a person. She remembers Jet arriving one night absolutely 'soaked' with ale demanding that she put the house on the market because he had no money for beer! He demanded half of the proceeds and to be left alone to live with Jackie.

With three youngsters to bring up, the answer was unprintable!

With so much going on, something had to crack. It was Jet. Suddenly his whole life flashed before him. He was rushed into hospital. Everybody expected the worst. He wasn't surprised at the outcome. Cirrhosis of the liver had been diagnosed. His affinity with the top shelf had 'pickled' his liver. It had packed up.

This removed the wind form his sails. He was to remain dry for the next six months. Maggie for all that had gone before, showed concern. She knew that it would only be a matter of time before he started again.

Jet's affair with Jackie affected Maggie very badly. He begged her not to tell anybody. In the beginning Maggie was beside herself. She had spoken to her doctor. She had not only lost her husband, but her work was beginning to suffer as well. Due to the stress that Jet had instigated, she was unable to continue with her work. Her sanity too was being questioned.

Jet admitted that he was a poor excuse for a man. There were so many things he did wrong. Maggie stayed in as long as she was able...in the end it was all too much. He recalled that they were returning late one night from Nottingham. He kept asking her to stop for he wanted a drink. She had the money but refused to let him waste it on beer. He went totally berserk and banged her head in anger. He continued to argue all the way back and on reaching Stratford was ordered from the car. Alcohol had begun to make him more violent towards life. He was now abusing someone who loved and cared for him. Once again he had left her in tears.

Prior to their eventual separation, things were really beginning to happen for them both. Jet had his photography and seemed to be making a reasonable living. He had taken on a partner during those early days. Neil Piper was to feel Jet's affinity with drink and money. Jet ended up owing him a tidy sum. Maggie remembers him coming round one night, demanding his cash. Maggie had none and invited him to go upstairs and take any of Jet's belongings in order to pay off his debt. Jet left Maggie virtually penniless. She too ended up having to sell things to survive; she sold his cameras.

Jet admitted that when he left that Christmas he left her with £43 to spend on toys and food. His earnings were sometimes in excess of £250 a week...most of which disappeared over the bar or went up in smoke. Alec was still hanging in there, but only just. He couldn't understand what was going on, and even he had his doubts as to whether Jet would survive.

Maggie for her part couldn't do anything. She could only sit back and say,' What a fine time to pick to have an affair'. She was certainly right. Jet had kicked the one person who had given him her life right in the teeth. Maggie remembers him coming home one night in his usual state. He thought he was going to die. Without warning, he suddenly passed out, swallowing his tongue. Maggie retrieved it with a spoon down his throat. He was again taken to Coney Hill. He survived the night. Jet discharged himself the following morning and went straight down the pub for a drink!

Maggie couldn't believe it when he rolled in some time later. She had rung the hospital to see how he was and was informed that he had 'checked' himself out. She knew by the state of him that he had once again 'checked in' at the local inn.

Affairs and alcohol go hand in hand. Deceitfulness is its own worst enemy. Its just lie after lie. Jet was ducking and diving from one bar to the next, from one woman to another. To him it was always easy come easy go. He always thought that because of who he was he could have his pick of anyone at a time to suit him. It never once entered Jet's head that he wasn't as popular as he'd thought he was. Jet admitted that he was an obnoxious little man and Maggie couldn't put up with it anymore.

Jet tried to put on as much decorum as the alcohol would allow. He knew that his body was beginning to waste away, but once you've got it, it won't let you go.

Maggie says", you could buy him the world and he would drink it"

He was beginning to clutch at straws. Maggie had got her life back in some sort of order, enough for her to return to work on a part-time basis. Maggie now had money coming in. Jet needed to drink that wage away. He would try and 'cadge' any money he could on every occasion.

The situation was now totally un-workable. Jet had to choose one or the other. Jet knew deep down that there weren't many women who could live up to Maggie. The early eighties gave Jet some of the most soul-searching times of his life. He had regained respect and some of his dignity from his photography, but he had now thrown that all away. Whatever his head should have told him, his heart lead the way...

He chose Jackie...

Jet and Jackie set up home at Jackie's in Beauford Road Matson, Gloucester. For good or bad the decision had been made. Having left prior to Christmas '85 had saved Jet the ignominy of having to face Maggie's mum and dad. Maggie even covered for him then, saying that he was working in Cheltenham.

Maggie says that perhaps if she had waited until after the birth of Craig, things might have been different. Throughout it all Maggie was his strength but Jet was too blind to see. For him it was par for the course. Jackie on the other hand had all this to come.

But she was the new lady in his life.

Jackie had had an office background and was pretty adept at general organisational skills and they decided that she should become his manager. She soon learned how to sell him. Within weeks she had started the ball rolling, taking telephone calls and making provisional bookings for the future. She was to rebuild the future of Jet Harris.

Jet always felt that perhaps Jackie wanted him for whom he was and what he might become and not for just plain Terry. The time with Jackie was going to be rather a little unstable. She had yet to handle the press.

Within weeks Jet was to have his name splashed all over the newspapers yet again. The Sun had hidden a photographer in Beauford Road, having heard about his split with Maggie. Jet and Jackie were out walking the dogs when Jet happened to stub his foot on the ground. Stumbling slightly, he thought nothing of it. The papers of course thought otherwise. Jet was dressed in an old duffel coat and the papers had given the impression that he was really down and out. Life on the dole and all that crap was all they could come up with.

The story about being on the dole was true. He had been earning money before he had met Jackie, but work wasn't too plentiful, and Jackie was trying her utmost to find it for him. Jet felt it only right that he should receive benefits from the state; after all he had paid enough in taxes during the sixties.

Jackie was working though only part-time. Jet did a little work on a couple of occasions. A scrap metal dealer took Jet on. It was bloody hard work tatting for scrap. Scrap dealers pull all sorts of stunts to earn extra money. Jet remembered being weighed in himself. The boss had asked him to climb under some scrap. They weighed in an extra eight and half stone!

Jet's worst experience during this period was his time working for an ice-cream company, Tartaglia's. They had a fleet of vans and were often to be seen on the streets of Gloucester. Jet recalled that he used to sell all sorts of weird and wonderful things, often sitting for hours not selling a thing. He would on occasions, enjoy the odd ice cream himself, so much so that he actually became addicted to it! He ended up getting frostbite in his fingers! He had the unique job of trying to sell ice-cream during the winter...he said 'it was like asking an

Eskimo if he needed any ice cubes!' His fingers would often turn black. Thawing them out after work in front of the fire was blessed relief!

Jackie's endeavours had paid off. Work was beginning to pick up. They began to travel the country. Jet put it down to Jackie's hard work. It was not drink, though the odd one or two did pass his lips behind her back! Jackie took charge of the finances. She used to give him pocket money, which ensured that he remained sober. If he hadn't got it, he couldn't drink it!

Jackie was to become his life.

Alec his roadie had taken a step backwards to allow him the space to get his life into order. He was still Jet's best mate in the months to come. For the moment life with Jackie can wait...

The next chapter is dedicated to him...

BUMHOLE....

Alec Merrick first met Jet in 1980. Alec had taken up employment with a company in Brimscombe about two miles out of Stroud. Jet too had managed to secure some work there and although still heavily into drinking turned up most mornings a little bit worse for wear. This particular morning after an especially bad session the night before had left him with a pretty bad head. Without warning he uttered 'bumhole!' after dropping something and the pair of them just burst into fits of hysterical laughter.

They hit it off almost immediately. They both had the same sense of humour. Jet had recently spent some time at an alcoholic clinic in Coney hill, a hospital on the outskirts of Gloucester. He had been advised to go on a rehabilitation course and needed to take his mind off the drink and occupational therapy seemed like the only viable option.

Marianne Electronics was situated within an old Cotswold stone building set beside a millpond. Jet had always had an interest in photography, and when time and the drink would allow he would often be found sitting beside the pond with his camera catching insects and birds on film. Alec would assist him carrying his cameras, tripods and the like from his car. Alec was totally enthralled by it all, and after many conversations on the subject,constantly encouraged Jet to this end.

It was a far cry from the Two 'I's' and the seedy streets of Soho and seemed to be a different world. Sometimes before and after work he would sit for hours waiting for the right moment to release the shutter.

Most lunch times would find him wandering up and down the canal bank trying to keep his mind occupied and keeping him out of the pub! Like many occasions before he would lapse into good and bad days. He drank in spasms. The therapy seemed to be working for he could go for weeks without alcohol and then suddenly something minor would trigger him off sending him straight down to the off licence.

Alec was to work alongside Jet for a couple of years. They were always laughing at something. The humour always seemed to be aimed at one fella in particular. He was the firms 'snitch' and nobody liked him. The firm produced fruit machines and on many occasions they used to hide in the wooden shells of these machines and shout out 'BUMHOLE as he passed by. The factory floor would also engage in the banter with Alex's voice ringing out like Harry Secombe. It was just like a Welsh Choir!

Jet used to pick Alec up along with a couple of other guys who lived in Stroud. Driving his car always meant taking extra care. His level of alcohol staying with him for most of the time never truly leaving his body and he was almost certainly beyond the legal limits every time he got into the car. Coney Hill for all its good intentions had placed him there for therapeutic reasons. Jet often abused this by sneaking out for a mid morning break which should have lasted ten minutes to return an hour later 'merrily' carrying on where he left off as if nothing had happened.

Jet was still residing with Maggie. He had met Jackie whilst at the clinic. They were friends but as yet not lovers. He was still managing to do the odd gig with a local outfit from Cheltenham 'The Strangers'. Alec came along one night acting as his 'roadie' he didn't need any firing up and within weeks he was 'roadying' for Jet.

The sixties seemed an eternity ago. Recording music just didn't happen. Tony Meehan rang suggesting that they get together and lay some tracks down. The phone call gave Jet a bit of a boost. Could this be the break he had been looking for after all this time. On the spur of the moment he threw in his job.

Alec wished him luck and Jet promised him work as his road manager when the work was completed. He seemed to like the idea. In reality Jet didn't see Alec again for nearly eighteen months. Alec was made redundant in 1983.

One Saturday afternoon Jet rolled up out of the blue at Alec's house. There was a UK tour starting that night and true to his promise asked him if he would like to do some driving. Being still out of work Alec didn't take too much persuading, it sounded good to him, and they hit the road.

Jet had managed to secure a spot on an 'Oh Boy' sixties package tour along with the Dallas Boys, the Vernon Girls, Heinz from the Tornado's and Eden Kane who topped the bill. The tour was to last three to four months. They returned home as and when time allowed. Alec needed to keep Jet reasonably sober during this first tour for if he did well a second was soon to follow.

Hal Carter, Billy Fury's ex roadie along with Henry Sellers had put another show together featuring Tommy Bruce, Dave 'Screaming Lord' Sutch and Ricky Valance. Hal and Henry were from Liverpool and stood no messing. Jet's new agent Norman Brodie had put his name forward after a reasonable report from the first tour and reputation apart Hal and Henry decided to take a chance.

Maggie and Jet were drifting further apart. Jackie had now taken more of an interest; in fact she had become his personal manager. Her beauty and presence always helped whenever she attended gigs and it did no harm to enhance Jet's struggling reputation.

Unlike the sixties there was no tour coach. All artistes had to make their own way to the venues. It was a case of see you tomorrow night. Most of the driving was done at night. People must have thought them crazy both Alec and Jet often dancing in the street at four or five in the morning! It was the only way of staying awake!

Hal was a stickler for punctuality. He insisted that all acts be at the venue by two in the afternoon. He needed to get the sound checks and rehearsals out of the way. Hal knew of Jet's reputation with the bottle telling Alec that if he smelled alcohol on him he would not perform that night and even worse, not get paid.

He was a hard taskmaster. He too had a reputation to uphold so took no prisoners. For that reason Jet stayed sober. What he did between gigs was his affair. Alec always ensured that he was fit to perform.

Alec remembered the first time he met Hal. He took him to one side at the Lakeside Club

'Keep him sober or no money'

Hal always insisted that Alec tell him if he had been drinking. Alec knew when and what to say for Hal would have no hesitation in walking on stage to inform the audience that Mr Harris was incapable of performing. Hal was the boss.

He certainly frightened Jet. He stayed sober for virtually the whole tour!

Heinz didn't help the cause. On one occasion he left Jet a double vodka behind the shower curtain in the dressing room. One gulp and he would be off again. Alec would check every possible hiding place for drink. On one occasion Jet actually had to pour it away under orders from Alec!

Maggie had put up with the brunt of his drinking for many years. One time whilst living in Cleveland Road, Gloucester he had been out on the binge. He had suffered with ulcers and this particular night they were giving him a lot of trouble.

Alec was also there. He remembers talking to him all night. He had to. Jet told Alec that he felt as if he was dying. Jet had been close to death on a couple of other occasions, but felt that this time he wasn't going to make it. Alec managed to get him through. Jet never seemed to heed any advice when it came to drinking. He never once thought of the damage that he was inflicting upon himself. Some months earlier he had received devastating news regarding his liver, but he continued to drink undeterred.

He always used to say,

'If I am going to go then I'm going to go happy'

Jet always defied doctor's orders. True he would recover for a while, feel fit and well so go out for a celebratory drink and off we would go again.

The package tours were a good tonic for him as they kept him in the public eye. If nothing else they had given him something to get out of bed for in the morning other than a can of ale. He had destroyed his life totally and no one wanted to know him. associate with him or take a chance on him.

Alec remembers probably the worst night of his career. Performing at Blazers Night Club he came on to do his spot. The opening tune being completely played in the wrong key! Chris Black and the Black Cats were doing their best to cover, Chris eventually turning Jet's amplifier off leaving Jet to go through the motions whilst he covered on guitar. Later that night Chris told Alec that he and the boys were not prepared to cover for him any longer. It wasn't good for their image. Through Jet's sheer incompetence he was not only losing work for himself but also for the band. with prospective booking agents sitting in the audience. To their defence most of the agents had turned up expecting Jet to be pissed but for the most part he was genuinely sober!

Jet's performance at the Lakeside stole the show. Alec recalls that he wasn't allowed out front. This also went for the crew and lady friends of the artistes; Hal always said that it was bad for their image. Hal told Alec that the fans still held Jet in very high esteem regardless of his antics off stage. He never let Hal down.

The green room provided a big screen on which to watch the rest of the acts on the show. This proved not only a learning tool but also a chance to assess your performance and that of the audience. The management had enforced the rule that no one but no one was allowed out front. Their fees were at stake. They all obeyed the rules.

Maggie and Jackie were the two women in Jet's life. He wasn't sleeping around. There was never any time for that. The schedules were hectic. Alec and Jet slept when and where they could. The travelling could put you at the Three Castles Club, Durham one night to find yourself at the Festival Hall, Paignton the next. Hal took care of all the expenses. Hotels and food when needed- they never wanted for anything.

The gig at the Three Castles found them both booked in at a hotel. Hal and the Vernon girls were already up and at breakfast. Alec and Jet sat in the bar area drinking orange juice. A young lady from reception joined them. She smiled and handed Jet a bill for £200! He looked in astonishment thinking that she expected him to settle it. He looked towards her turning a little white.

Alec said, 'what's up?'

Alec suggested that he take the bill over to Hal. Alec made his way over to their table. Telling Hal that Jet was in a bit of a state over this money Hal replied,

'Just tell Mr Harris to sit in the bar and look famous'

The travelling was becoming a real challenge. Maggie and Jackie got the occasional telephone call home as did Alec's wife. It was make do on someone's couch if need be. Staying at home had become a bit of a rarity and only happened when they were in easy reach of home.

Jet had worked with almost everybody there was to know during his career. He recalled a funny story that happened one night. He was working alongside a famous group of singing brothers. One of the brothers had always fancied taking a young lady whilst she was looking out of a window waving to people below. Well there he was making love to her from the back with her leaning out of the window smiling and waving to the folks below. Making an excuse that he wanted to use the toilet and would be back in a minute he told her to stay where she was and not to move. Unbeknown to her his brother came out from the wardrobe and took over. Still unaware and waving from the window the original brother emerged in the street waving back up to her! Her face was a picture!

Alec had recorded Duane Eddy's 'Guitar Man' and Jet agreed that it would be a good tune to do with the girls doing the vocals hidden behind a curtain. Whilst rehearsing, a member of another act on the bill appeared from the toilet with his tackle in his hand beside them. One of the girls said,

'I've just got through three verses of this tune and I've just realised that I haven't been singing into the mic!

The other girls tried hard to keep a straight face but they all broke down in fits of the giggles. There was always someone ready to wind someone up!

Alec and Jet shared a battered old Marina. A bit of an old banger, but it did the job. On the way to a job at Peppermint Park, Warrington, just north of Birmingham the car started to knock. They managed to 'nurse' her up to the gig and weren't looking forward to the return journey. Leaving the theatre around one thirty in the morning they started the exceptionally slow trek back home. Reaching junction 2 on the M6 just south of Walsall they were joined by a police car. The car had followed them for some miles noticing that they were only doing fifteen to twenty miles an hour. Pulling over they must have thought that the occupants of the car had had a few. Jet was asleep in the back Alec winding down the window explaining who they were and where they were going. They had to get to Paignton that night. The police weren't interested and said sorry for bothering them and just left them to it.

Seven hours later and they eventually reached Gloucester. Alec had had no sleep. Paignton was still some 160 miles away. Jet managed to trade in the car for a slightly newer one, Alec telling him not to go over the top just to get something economical. He came back from Taylor's in Gloucester with a bloody great Volvo!Economical no, but very reliable .It did the job well until one day when Jet had had a little too much to drink and promptly smashed into the back of someone at a roundabout. The court appearance removed his licence. Alec and Jackie were now the only way of getting to the gigs.

Jet was earning around £200 a night working four nights a week. Jackie was now well into her 'manage-ment' demanding that Alec 'tip' over the money when she found herself on the road with them. She would give out 'expenses' like pocket money for the week. It kept Jet away from the bar.

He never knew where all that money went.

Maggie was beginning to fade further away. Her three children had to take preference over everything. When the tours ended he was without work. Inevitably he drifted back to the bar. Maggie had suspected that Jackie was after a little more than she had imagined. Jet and Jackie were growing closer. Maggie had always treated her as a friend since Jet's time in Coney Hill 'drying' out where he met her. The drink had turned Maggie off. He wanted the love of a good woman. He had already got that from Maggie his wife of fifteen years. He was too blind to see it. Jackie seemed to be the only one giving him solace. She gave him protection. Alcohol was again blinding his vision. He started to spend more time away from Mafeking. Maggie knew that if he didn't come home, she knew where he'd be. Unbeknown to Jet it was breaking her heart.

Maggie accepted the inevitable.

Jackie was like a Svengali figure. She had him dangling. Maggie always kept her faith in Alec and always felt reassured whenever he was with Jet. But his involvement had nothing to do with their marriage and the way it was falling apart.

Jet moved in with Jackie.

Jet had met Jackie in Coney Hill. She had already suffered a breakdown and at the time her own marriage was in trouble. She lived with her two children in

Matson a suburb of Gloucester and she too had started to get a little frustrated with the business and Jet's attitude. Because of his affliction with the bottle the booze and stardom or visions of it she too would sometimes go a little off line. In a fit of rage she cut up all of his clothes, all because he had gone round to see Maggie and his boys. Maggie had filed for divorce. They still had to communicate. Jackie didn't like it.

Alec didn't go with them to Cliff's biggest gig 'The Event' at Wembley Stadium. There was no need for him to go. Without Maggie it was Jackie who went to the show. She loved the smell of stardom. She was surrounded by the rich and famous. She was a little more than envious of the attention he was receiving.

Alec too was beginning to get entangled in the mess that Jet had caused with his relationship with Maggie. Jackie had got to the point of stopping Jet from going anywhere near the cottage. Jet wanted to pick up some of his personal memorabilia he had amassed over the years. Alec got lumbered with that job. He was the go between. Maggie would tell him that Jackie had already been up and taken them. Alec took her to one side. He had to have it out with her. Jackie admitted that she had taken his personal belongings and sold them!

Jackie was very formidable. Jet always seemed to follow in her shadow. The drinking was once again getting out of hand. Alec had to book him into the clinic for another 'drying' out session. Jet had in fact asked Alec on a couple of occasions to do it for him; Alec knew when enough was enough.

Alec recalls that on numerous occasions Jet would emerge from the clinic as bright as a button only to blow it within days. It nearly came to a head one day when Alec had suffered a personal tragedy within his household. Jet arrived at the door 'tanked' up. Alec who was stricken with grief answered the door. Jet burst in going on about his problems completely oblivious of the state of Alec and his wife and kids.

Alec, like the guy he is, put his own problems to one side and took him into Coney Hill yet again. Alec told him straight. That was it; it had to be sorted once and for all. Maybe that was pure frustration but he had had enough. Helping him so many times Jet still kept coming back for more. Every time he would abuse the help, he even asked Alec if he could have a drink on the way in!

It didn't really matter for Jet just sat in the back giggling. He had hidden four cans under the seat. The insensitivity of it all. Jet was totally unaware. That's what alcohol does. Eventually they reached the hospital. Jet told Alec he could go now. Alec was having none of it. He stayed to make sure that he actually booked himself in.

Jet stayed for four days.

His confidence was now at its lowest ebb. On this occasion he managed to get it right. It was to be his last visit to the clinic. The hospital never took him in again. He was wasting their time.

A broken man. He had always thrown back the help offered into people's faces. His mouth had always got him into some sort of trouble. Alec was surprised that no one had knocked his head off his shoulders. Making allowances for the liquor wasn't enough. Jet was obnoxious and rude to the point of distraction. He carried this 'rebel' image from his days with the Shadows. It was no surprise really after all he seemed to self-destruct every so often. Getting right was easy; keeping it right was almost impossible.

Alec stayed with Jet for nearly seven years, enjoying many laughs together. Alec remembers touring with the late Tommy Bruce. Sitting at the bar one day, Tommy ordered a Pina Colada. Sitting back relaxing he waited patiently for his drink to arrive. Tommy had already tried a similar drink Malibu and coconut during one of the earlier tours and fancied trying another exotic cocktail. The waitress who had seemed to be gone for ages suddenly appeared with a glass filled with umbrellas and things. He couldn't contain himself and with his inimitable cockney accent replied,

'Where have you been for that f-----g Jamaica, I ordered a drink not a tropical rain forest!'

As Alec says, that was Tommy to a T - full of charm and elegance! Another time whilst waiting for Dave Sutch to arrange the running time for the night, Tommy again was his usual carefree happy self. As time went by he said....

'Where the f—k is he? I'll give him f-----g Screaming Lord Sutch!'

Alec recalls that all the artistes had their own way of warming up for the shows. The Dallas Boys would walk around in a circle loosening up their vocal chords sometimes to the tune of BumHoleeee...

Leighton Summers who took off Elvis, always maintained he needed eight hours sleep prior to the gig. He would always lock himself away in his dressing room and on occasions, he too was heard walking up and down the corridor singing Bumhole!

Women were always at hand, some more available than others. Alec and Jet had theirs at home. It was the time of their lives. Jet had somehow clawed his way back from the jaws of death to again savour the taste of success. The shows were always sell-outs. Jackie was still handing out his pocket money. The more he earned the more he appeared to give away. Complete strangers would find themselves at the bar, sharing a drink or three!

Hal Carter too took his fair share of ribbing. Alec remembers Jet calling the waitress over one day and asking her to give a note he had written previously to the big man as they sat waiting for the evening meal. Hal was seated alongside the Vernon girls and Eden Kane.

The note read...

Dear Mr. Carter

We value your custom very much and are pleased that you are staying at our hotel. We have noticed that you have been to the toilet, and unfortunately your dress has not been adjusted correctly. Please rearrange your dress as your brooch and earrings are hanging over the chair... ps... I love you...

Hal stood up and looked down at his flies. All was well. Looking across towards Jet and Alec he replied 'you bastards!' much to the amusement of his table.

Mike Berry too has experienced the effects of Jet's love affair with the bottle. Alec remembers a night when Jet was on the same bill along with Ricky Valence just outside Oxford. Mike had another gig to go to and asked Alec if Jet would like to 'guest' at his next gig the following evening in Southport. Alec couldn't see any problem and promised to get him there. Returning back to Gloucester Jet booked into the Downfield Hotel, Stroud and hit the sack.

Alec returned around lunchtime to pick him up. He was legless. Alec couldn't move him. The owner of the hotel who knew of Jet's problems had rang for an ambulance during the night, actually fearing that he was about to die. Alec rang Mike, who said, 'just get him here, we'll get him on somehow.'

Jet had hit the vodka as soon as he reached his room. He couldn't get off the bed. Alec again rang Mike. He was so ill he couldn't walk. Mike understood. Alec immediately rushed him into Coney Hill. He was still in their 'good' books at the time and he was duly admitted. Mike was bitterly disappointed with Jet. Not only had he let himself down once again, he had also let both Mike and Alec down too.

Alec was always there to pick up the pieces once again. The excuses that he had to make seemed endless. He was constantly being knocked over to pick himself up and try and put Jet's situation back on track. Jackie too had little concept of the deadlines that had to be met. Hal was a stickler for timekeeping. Travelling to gigs Alec had to get used to her ways, stopping at the first services that they came too. To her it was just like a picnic. Both Alec and Jet could see where she was going wrong, but kept it buttoned both being too frightened to voice an opinion for fear of the consequences and words that might transpire on the way home.

The last thing Alec wanted was for Jet to panic. Alec knew that if that happened he would surely find the bottle again to steady his nerves. Jackie and Jet were too much alike. Alec knew that on occasions Jet was too frightened to return home. Jackie for all her influence was slowly burning him out.

Alcoholism is a disease. It destroys the brain cells. It destroys life. Jet would do anything for a beer, thinking nothing of buying a guitar one week to trade it in the next for the entrance fee into the next boozer. He would always tell himself that he needn't worry, if he happened to be working that night then he would just borrow another guitar. Alec recalled that he remembered Jet had taken nearly three hundred pounds for one instrument to find the money gone within five days!

Jet had no fear or regard for anything or anyone during these dank days, doing anything to satisfy his need. Alcohol is a drug.

During this period of his life he met up with Cliff's sister, Donna. Their brief relationship gave him hope. Maybe he read too much between the lines. Jet had always held a candle for her ever since those early days back in the sixties. But it was the 80's not the 60's everybody growing older and some more wiser. They always seemed to have a mutual 'love' for each other. Donna became the distraction that was needed to remove the temptation to drink his life away. She became another 'crutch' for him to lean on. Their time together was precious.

For the most part the touring kept Jet sober. Alec seemed never to be out of the company of Hal Carter and his entourage. Hal always chaperoned the 'star' of the show. Eden Kane seemed to fit the bill having had a string of hits. Well I Ask You (Decca F11353) his first recording reaching number one in June 1961 staying in the charts for twenty-one weeks. His next four releases all made the top ten, Get Lost (Decca F11381) reaching number ten September 1961, Forget Me Not (Decca F11418) number three in January 1962, I Don't Know Why (Decca F11460) climbing to number seven in May of that year. His last real shot at the charts Boys Cry (Fontana TF438) making number eight in January 1964.

One of Alec's favourites was Heinz of Just Like Eddy fame his only real success also released by Decca (F11693) attaining the dizzy heights of number five in August 1963. His involvement with the legendary Joe Meek with whom he shared a flat always gave the impression that he came across as a gay person but he was a dead straight guy. Alec remembers that he would always appear at the theatres with the same young lady on his arm. He was one of the boys.

Alec had the pleasure of meeting the great late Jerry Lordan one afternoon before a gig. Jerry lived in North Wales and because of his involvement with The Shadows especially Apache he and Jet had remained good friends for many years. Alec found him the most unassuming man to the point of being shy. He loved his home-made wine. Alec had no problem downing a few whilst Jet remained on lemonade!He had a show to do that night.

Billie Davies had told Alec sometime before that Jet was bloody hard work. Way back from her days in the sixties when they were an item she always had to try to keep him focussed. Alec worked damn hard to keep Jet at the top. Jet always held Alec in high esteem although he never really appreciated what he used to do for him due to alcohol being just around the corner.

During his time at Marianne's Electronics, Alec took a telephone call from Jackie. They had acquired a new car, a bright red Ford Capri, and they had been involved in an accident. Jackie asked him to drop everything and come and drive them back home to Gloucester. Downing his tools Alec obliged. On his arrival Alec was fuming. Jet was totally pissed and unable to drive and to his amazement Jackie had taken the wheel of the car without a licence and worse still not knowing how to drive the bloody thing! She had in her infinite wisdom, collided with the rear end of a truck. After wangling his way out of work that afternoon he managed to get the vehicle back for repair. All Jackie had to say was,

'Someone had to drive'

The car remained with Alec for the time being. It came as a bit of a surprise to him when one day out of the blue Jet rolled up with his uncle from London. The car had to go back... they hadn't paid for it!

The original repair costing slightly more than he had bargained for due to Jet getting 'stroppy' with the owner who was a friend of Alec's telling him,

'Don't you know who I am!'

Once again the drink was talking. He told them to take it elsewhere. They did and it cost them a lot more.

The addiction to alcohol or drugs seems part and parcel of the music business. Anybody who's anybody seemed to have indulged in one way or the other. Alec recalls that the late John Walker from the Walker Brothers suffered the same way as Jet. They were doing a week at Blazers. The word was out that John's wife was in town and on her way over. She hated the way he was. Covering all entrances everybody was doing the utmost to sober him up before she arrived. Dave Sutch desperately working his arse off in John's dressing room. Somehow they got it together. A few weeks later, after John had returned to the States, Alec and Jet received a letter from his wife thanking them for looking after him during the tour.

The late Tommy Bruce never minced his words. Alec was sitting with him one day at Dingwalls club when Jess Conrad 'breezed' in. Tommy was right on form that day. Jess, known as Prince Charming because of his 'eternal' looks,

'I'll give him Prince F-----g Charming, I think I'll rip his head off and shit in the hole!'

Jess and Tommy obviously had some misgivings. Jess wasn't appearing there, he had only popped in to say hello! Voted the most popular male vocalist of 1963 he is best remembered for Mystery Girl (Decca F11315) charting at 18 in February 1961. His first release Cherry Pie (Decca F11236) only reached number 39 in June 1960. His last release Pretty Jenny (Decca F11511) ended up at number 50 in October 1962.

Alec would sometimes send orders out to the bouncers from Jet asking for certain young ladies to be 'bathed and scrubbed and sent his room immediately after the show!'

Jet. as the story goes once got stuck in a room with a guy by the name of Roger Byron a 'raging queen' Roger had offered Jet the use of his spare room. They had met up during a gig some years earlier. This particular night Roger had taken his boyfriend home. Jet was awoken in the night by the moaning sounds of

'Struth Roger, go gently!'

Alec and Jet shared many lovely moments together. They had a special relationship. Being associated with the showbiz world, and Alec himself was a pretty mean drummer; the other stars treated him like one of their own. On one occasion the 'Oh Boy' show had to do a couple of nights in Jersey. Alec was all set to go. Jet received a telephone call telling them that the hotels in question had their own crews for the shows. The disappointment was evident but was offset when the Dallas Boys who knew Alec as a friend presented him with one of their albums, Love Is A Many Splendoured Thing, signed personally as a token of their friendship. Alec didn't only care for Jet he cared for others too. He remains the same today.

Whenever Alec bumped into Mr Harris as he did on a regular basis the strains of

BUM...HOLLLLLE... would ring out.

Alec always held a special place in Jet's life,

He is one of the boys.

CATCH A FALLEN STAR..

Life with Jackie had begun to take on a different meaning. Maggie although only a few miles away had conditioned herself to the prospect of spending the rest of her life without Jet. She was always a very big part of his life even though life at that time was a little more than hazy. Like all new relationships, things didn't go quite as smoothly as he expected.

Within weeks of moving in with Jackie, he declared himself bankrupt. Owing around ten thousand pounds, a lot of money in the eighties didn't make life any easier. He had 'wasted' for want of a better word the best part of whatever income he had over the bar. Life with Maggie although a little strained at times at least gave him the comfort of his wife, children and his memories. Maggie worked as a nurse and her income had become the only real main source of any income. Jet worked as and when, now it was if he were able to work. Jet had tried desperately to keep it together. He was getting deeper and deeper into trouble. However much he tried to keep afloat the further he swam against the tide. It just wasn't working.

Jet attributed most of his debts to bad business debts and loans and was now hoping that Jackie could stem the tide and help him get through the hard times that were inevitably lying ahead.

The courts immediately swallowed up any income, and worse was to follow, having to contend with the loss of his driving licence due to drink.

He still clung on to his memories. He had his gold disc along with two silver ones to remind him that there were good times. But that was twenty years before and his life had moved on albeit a little wayward to the normal pathway.

Jackie had welcomed Jet into her home. Jackie's children didn't really care for him too much being like most kids, very protective of their mother. Both in their teens they shared the house together with two dogs. The move ensured that she had complete control over every move he made. She was full time management, throwing herself into the business at every opportunity.

Jackie was becoming Jet Harris.

Jackie always meant well. Rebuilding Jet's career especially at the low ebb he had sunken to, meant dedication all the way. Someone had to do it nobody else really wanted to know. Within three months the novelty of the new woman was beginning to wear off. Jet was becoming totally stifled. To the outside world all seemed well, behind closed doors many rows were to follow in the year to come. Being with Jackie didn't give Jet too much time to drink. She made sure of that, although she occasionally hit the bottle. Many times Jet would just go to bed early to get out of it only to come down stairs to find her well and truly 'tanked' up.

Jet wanted desperately to beat the alcohol Could you imagine pouring drink down the kitchen sink…no, not for his benefit, but to stop her from getting drunk! Although not addicted to the drink like Jet it didn't seem to matter a jot when she herself was on it. She had her moments. The domination was at times unbearable, on one occasion tying him to the banister of the stairs with a rope around his neck to stop him from going out. Most of his belongings were already at the house in Beauford Road. Matson. He was beginning to think if he had made the right decision leaving Maggie. Maggie had always been beside him whatever the situation, leaving her for Jackie seemed easy. Jackie was beautiful. He fully believed that she was all he had ever wanted.

Life continued with Jackie working hard to secure as much work as she could. A double hernia was to slow him down and following his operation on the 11th October 1987, he managed to play at Stringfellows Hippodrome in London. He really hadn't fully recovered from the surgery but still managed to squeeze in another gig at the BAC Club, in Bristol. Not liking to panic, as Jet's nerves have always been a problem he was due to use Chris Black and the Black Cats. Chris had been taken ill. Jet started to panic but managed to see the night through being joined on stage by Terry Dene.

A ten-day tour of Scandinavia had been organised with Jackie and Jet due to fly out at the beginning of November. Due to circumstances beyond their control this was cancelled at the last minute, although they did take in one gig in Sweden at the Friends Meeting Place. Terry Dene joining them.

Bo Laarson and Jan Lyckman who ran a local studio over there, invited Terry and Jet to put some tracks down for a possible new album release in 89. Nothing ever came of this Jet eventually returning to England to start work on his Anniversary album at Muff Murfin's studios in Kempsey. Muff had taken an interest in Jet and seemed like the right guy to promote his career especially now after making real efforts to shake the bottle.

Jackie was optimistic. Jet was on the up. He managed to do three radio interviews and one television all in one day! With the new album well under way it looked to all intents and purposes that the bad days were well and truly behind him. He threw himself into the recording sessions with great gusto. Tangent, the Bristol Shadows, accompanied Jet throughout December taking in Cheltenham Town Hall, The Common Wheel in Swindon and an unannounced appearance at the Oasis Club, Porth Rhondda on Boxing Day.

January was the lull after the storm only managing to do one gig at the Frimley Community Centre. Jackie had suggested putting together his own band. This wasn't a problem, but he stuck with the guys who were covering the gigs already. They knew the routine.

Terry Dene's wedding came midway through the month and an impromptu appearance at the reception was the least that he could do. Jackie had managed to secure a run of gigs, February and March both picking up. Kidderminster and the Wimbledon Theatre working alongside Chris Black soon followed. Twist and Shout were to provide the backing at Greenford, Middlesex, but Jet had had second thoughts about what Jackie had suggested, still hankering after his own band.

Through the endeavours of Jackie, Jet seemed to be always working, being invited by the Dallas Boys, Craig Douglas, The Vernon Girls and the Bash Band to guest alongside them on a twenty date tour during March and April. The tour over it was back to the rounds. April 22nd found Jet working at Crystals, Newtown South Wales, finishing off the month with Tangent at the Coral Show Bar, Torquay. The Dallas Boys tour took its toll; an injury to his ribs prevented him from completing the final three gigs. Within weeks he was back to full strength working with Tommy Bruce and Love Affair at Strood in Kent. The Assembly Rooms Melksham quickly followed with Mike Berry and the Rapiers.

Jet was suddenly in demand. The odd charity fundraiser found its way into the diary. His sporting days being well and truly over he decided to try his hand one day at golf at St. Giles Golf Club Newtown Powys. Reg Thomas. Ken Smart and John Morgan partnered Jet helping him 'hack' his way around the course! For his noble efforts that day, he was presented with a car stereo and a small trophy at the dinner later that evening at the Elephant and Castle. An impromptu appearance with the local band followed.

Jet tried to put a band together but working with Tangent who had become his main source of backing meant that he couldn't give it the time or energy that it deserved. Tangent knew his ins and outs. Alec and Jackie continued to ferry him all over the country. The year had suddenly gone and Scandinavia once again beckoned. It meant only a week away being backed by a local band The Beatniks, consisting of; Sevin Finjarn-guitar, Carstan Deberitz-bass, Odvar Gunderson-Guitar and John Truls Lorck on drums. The tour was to take in six venues during September, firstly Fredrikstad on the 13th followed by Oslo on the 14th, Sarpsbenge on the 15th, Son 16th, Langsuub 17th finishing at Tarsby on the 18th. The week went well, Jet and Jackie being made welcome wherever they went. November found him in Holland. The Dutch group F.B.I. doing the honours for a one off gig at the Theater Noorderlist in Tilberg.

The first year with Jackie had gone reasonably well. Although he wasn't truly happy with her and still harboured the odd thought for Maggie, she had done him proud. Jet found himself at the Osterley Hotel near Heathrow guesting for the Piper Alfa Appeal Disaster Fund charity concert organised by an old mate of his Robbie Mac. Cliff Bennett, Jess Conrad, Vanity Fayre, Terry Dene, Wee Willie Harris, Dave Sutch and Don

Lang. It was a night to renew some old friendships, especially with Don whom he had worked with some forty years before!

Jet and Jackie spent their first real Christmas together. It had been a gruelling twelve months, but with her persistence it had been a reasonably successful one. Jet was revelling in his new found romance with Jackie, but felt deep down that all was maybe going 'too' well. He wasn't going to rock the boat. His drinking was now virtually non-existent. The press still took an interest in his affairs, but he took it all in his stride.

January 1989 found him once again working for Robbie Mac in a production created by Robbie, The Story of Rock 'n' Roll at the Hammersmith Les Palais. The usual crew were there along with Marty Wilde, Lonnie Donegan, Gerry and the Pacemakers, The Troggs, Vanity Fayre and Showaddywaddy. The veteran DJ's Alan 'fluff' Freeman, David Jacobs and Stuart Coleman, hosted the show.

Jet had well and truly got the bit between his teeth and February found him at the Golden Cross, Slough, the Prison Officers Club, Ashford and the Marlow Theatre Canterbury. Twist and Shout once again providing the backing, Marc Lundquist-lead guitar, Chris Underhill on bass and Martin Symonds on drums. Martin and Jet had already met, Martin sitting in on Diamonds on the 'Legends' album. An appearance at the Fairwater Sports and Social club in Cwmbran followed backed by a local unnamed band featuring Gordon John-lead guitar, Rob Anderton –bass and Dave Clark on drums.

Jet and Jackie found themselves back on his favourite island in March. A gig at the White Cliff Bay Holiday Camp on the Isle of Wight along with Mike Berry. Jet remembered the gig well, receiving a 'huge' teapot enabling them both to have a warming cuppa!

The mid Wales Festival took pride of place over three days in mid April. A whole galaxy of stars were appearing including The Fourmost, Dave Sampson, Dave Berry, The Merseybeats, Fred the Ted, and Tommy Bruce. A couple of gigs followed at the Herton Staff Club, Malden and the George Inn at Petersfield, before a short hop over the channel to Holland to perform on the 29th with a Dutch band The Arrows.

Whenever Jet and Jackie went overseas, the tours always threw up new bands. The Arrows were no exception. They were probably one of the tightest outfits to work with Jet. Mastered by sound technician Rob Aartsen, Arie De Byrne who organised the gig played bass, accompanied by Fred Zevenbergen – drums, Jan Koining –rhythm and Cor Vielvoye on Lead guitar. The band also featured Peter V Hal on vocals.

Immediately after their return Jet and Jackie were heading off to Southsea. Jet seemed to be working every week. Jackie had ensured that he didn't remain idle. She always seemed to want more. True, she had given him direction, but her constant need for more was beginning to get Jet down. He didn't want to let it show. He would often sit and wonder just where his life was taking him. Having had minimal contact with Maggie and his boys during the last twelve months, the magic between him and Jackie was beginning to wear a little thin. He enjoyed the new found fame but he felt that he was beginning to fade - the travelling had begun to take its toll.

Just when he wasn't expecting it, a telephone call from Cliff Richards office came through. Cliff had been toying with the idea of putting on an extravaganza at Wembley Stadium. He had apparently been trying to find Jet for some time. Jet's eyes lit up. The show was to take the form of a sixties set coupled with Cliff's new routine. Cliff didn't have to ask twice. Within a week Jet and Jackie were on their way to London to speak to Cliff.

A week away in Benidorm mid May proved the right tonic. They both needed it. On their return it was straight into rehearsals for the new show.

The Event was to become the biggest rock and roll show with the exception of Band Aid. Booking into the Hilton Hotel just down the road from the stadium he was savouring the lifestyle. Jackie too was lapping up the atmosphere. The sound checks were carried out on the Thursday and Friday, prior to the show, and although Jet was only doing one tune with Cliff it was still a major undertaking. It had to be right.

The show enabled Jet to catch up with some old mates from the sixties; Hank, Bruce and Brian Bennett were there as was Tony Meehan with whom Jet was to perform. The Shadows were due to appear but due to a disagreement with the billing they refused. Jet and

Jackie soaked it up. Jet hadn't performed in front of so many people at one time. The two nights the show went out attracted 142,000 people. For Jet it was a very emotional time. Although not completely out of the woods regarding his drinking he managed to stay perfectly sober for the two days he was needed. Cliff was very warm and genuinely pleased to see him after all those years. The affair with Carol was now a thing of the past. It was time to forgive and forget. It was the most amazing thing Jet had ever done.

Jet remembered the finale as one of the most moving he had ever seen. Cliff finished the show with Julie Gold's classic, From A Distance. Singing it live the first night the emotion that it had on Cliff meant that he had to mime on the final night.

All the acts were personally chaperoned, wherever they went. The main control had to know where everybody was at any given time. Jet and Tony took to the stage with Cliff with the song that started it all off.. Move It. It was just like old times. Jackie had ensured that Jet would only drink orange juice for the two days, making sure that he would remain dry!

The show seemed to bring Jet and Jackie a little closer. She was thrilled for him and fitted in easily with all that was going on around her. Back stage in the Green Room it was like a school reunion. Some of the acts hadn't met each other in over thirty years! Cliff was impeccable. Donna his sister was there too. Jet had always had a secret longing for her and when they met they smiled and embraced each other without thinking. Jackie just looked on. That embrace was to lead to a national newspaper headline a little later.

Sitting around a table they talked of the old times. Donna was a fully-grown woman now, and not Cliff's 'little' sister from all those years back. It had been an open secret that Jet had always found Donna very attractive and if she hadn't had been so young all those years ago, who knows what might have happened... As the conversation progressed, Jackie was becoming a little agitated with Jet's 'advances' towards Donna. She had gotten hold of the wrong end of the stick. Donna was married. Jet was with Jackie. Jackie thought that Jet was turning his attention to Donna.

Returning home to Gloucester they said their goodbyes and promised to stay in touch. Donna had talked of a possible book. The idea appealed immediately to Jet, and they just left it at that. The adrenalin was still buzzing days after the show. This was the first real stepping stone for thirty years. Both he and Jackie needed to seize it with both hands.

Jet's fiftieth birthday was fast approaching. The Parkside Hotel, Bristol brought many friends both past and present for the celebration. Dave Holbrook and Dave Wheatley who had started up his fan club organised the get together via their monthly newsletter. The two 'Daves' along with Jackie had devoted their time to keeping members informed of his whereabouts and even through bouts of illness and family misfortune had managed to keep it going. They more than anyone deserved the night to be a success.

Baz Weaver hosted the night. Twist and Shout and The Rapiers provided the music entertaining many friends from all over the land including a party from Scandinavia. The only thing that didn't go according to plan was the buffet laid on for special guests... the fans got in first and scoffed the lot!

The Event was already recorded and ready to go out at Christmas. Donna as promised called Jet and they agreed to meet up to discuss the book in more detail. Jackie wasn't happy; she thought that Donna was after him, showing so much attention after all those years surely there was more to it than just a book?

Jet unknowingly was to pay for it.

The meeting passed and still nothing seemed to have come out of it. The distance between Jet and Jackie was growing, jet keeping his distance on more days than not, often just staying in bed out of it. It seemed to do the trick. The last few months had been gruelling and he needed to recharge his batteries. Six weeks had passed since the show at Wembley and once again work came trickling in. Norman Jay had suddenly taken an interest after his success appearing with Cliff. Norman ran a band called Vintage. He had suggested that they get together and gig with each other. Jet had first met up with Norman way back in August 1978.

During this period Jet received the news of the death of Sam Curtis the Shadows roadie. Sam was a marvellous character - Jet sharing good and bad times with him on the road. Sam put the origin Jet Blacks together back in the sixties. Barry Kenny on lead, Terry Webster bass, Quincy Davies Tenor Sax, Glen Hughes bass sax, and Mike Wonderwood on drums. Jet said you either loved Sam or hated him... he had a line for everybody famous or not. He took no notice of whom you were.

Tangent, the Bristol Shadows were still performing. Dave Bill and Mervyn Jeffries made up the line-up. Mervyn affectionately known as 'Merve the Swerve' was highly rated for his bass playing. They were always a safe bet when working with Jet, they knew his routine inside out. Jackie suggested that they maybe run an advert in The Stage offering a show. The advert had drew some attention and work began to come in. The shows to Jet weren't as important as the 'big one' he had just completed. He began to slip back into the old routine. The anticipated success that he thought might have elevated him back into the spotlight hadn't really materialised. He was just another working muso endlessly on the road.

Things back in Matson were getting too much. Something had to crack. Jet and Jackie parted company. For good or bad Jet had decided that he wanted to handle his own affairs from then on.

The end came within a month. A gig at Feltham Remand Centre with Twist 'n' Shout on the 1st September followed by one on the 2nd at Clevedon Football Club was the beginning of the end. He just went out one night on a gig and never came back.

Jet couldn't fault Jackie for all her faults. The public wanted more, she didn't. She just wanted Jet to herself.

She was pulling all the strings. Jet wanted none of it, there was nowhere left to go, he ate humble pie... he rang Maggie.

It was 1989. Maggie and Jet had been divorced for nearly twelve months. She had a new man in her life Norman R------had moved into Mafeking. Norman was an OK sort of guy and seemed to get a kick out of being associated with Jet. Maggie didn't really want him back, but after discussing it with Norman she agreed to put him up for the time being in a caravan at the bottom of the garden.

For Jet this was to almost be the last straw. To be living in a caravan alongside the house that evoked so many memories was devastating. Not only had he lost his direction the final insult was that Maggie whom he had never really stopped loving was now 'shacked' up with someone else in his house! He started to go steadily down hill. The gigs became less and the drinking became once again the norm. A feeling of complete despair descended. Four months before the euphoria of The Event and now total desolation.

His descent into drunkenness was a formality. He would emerge from the van looking like a zombie. He felt close to death. Maggie was right in the middle. She still cared for Jet. Jackie was throwing her weight about, refusing him access to her house. Jet still had a guitar along with his cameras, clothes and records to collect. She refused to give them to him. Norman had even asked for the police to intervene but they were powerless. They too were refused access. Offensive phone calls were now coming in on a regular basis. Maggie took all the crap.

Jackie wanted Jet Harris.

Terry Harris is all Jet wanted to be.

The last eighteen months had produced so much and yet he was left with so little. For all his faults he and Maggie then were still together for her and her alone was the only really true person who knew how to handle such a wayward person.

Around that time Jet had made the acquaintance of another muso Mike Porterfield originally from the Midlands but living in Cornwall. Mike was up that weekend working for Jet's agent Norman Brodie.

Mike called into Norman's office to find Jet sitting beside Norman. Norman asked Mike if he could use a bass player and he replied 'I might be able to'. Mike had recognised Jet who was sporting a beard at the time and with time to spare before the evening gig went back to Mafeking for the afternoon. It was a start of a friendship that would last for years.

Mike had been working at a pub called The Wellington off Cromwell St in Gloucester the previous evening and had stayed over at a B&B just down from the pub. One of the locals who lived in Cromwell St, John Harris invited him to Sunday lunch. The young lady who cooked and served the food wasn't the slimmest of creatures. Jet remembered how she told him that she defrosted the beefburgers under her arms! Jet telling her to cancel the hotdog! Norman and Jet both laughed and for the next few years all the correspondence between them revolved around food!

Like all musicians the conversation had to get round to music. Mike had written a couple of tunes - one that was to become one of Jet's favourite melodies, 'Here I Stand' the tune being lodged with a publishing company in Cornwall. Mike promised to send Jet a copy. Parting company they were not to speak or meet up again until some months later.

Jet and Maggie received a postcard one day. It was from Mike. He was out in Abu Dhabi on a three-month contract. Maggie had fallen in love with the tune. Jet who had previously moved in with Jackie still hankered after spending time with her, decided to give Muff Murfin a call regarding the tune. Muff decided that it was a strong contender for a comeback single and went ahead recording it on the Anniversary Album. Mike was unaware as to the developments with regard to the recording he was still overseas.

Jet and Muff decided to call the tune 'Jacqueline' after 'guess who!'. With the tune safely in the can Jet tried to contact Mike. He hadn't been long back from the Emirates and every time Jet tried to call he wasn't in. Finally Jet got through to tell him the good news. Meanwhile the company who retained the tune in Cornwall weren't happy about the 'infringement' that occurred with regard to recording. Muff was an experienced record producer and Mike being the writer didn't seem to pose any major problem with regard to the other company's involvement. The recording went ahead whilst Mike was overseas.

The comeback single wasn't to be.

Muff who had produced the album had to scrap every one. The Anniversary Album never came out. The track was on the album and the cost of re-recording was out of the question. The other company left Muff and Jet little alternative other than to withdraw the tune. It was to lie dormant until 2002.

This period in Jet's life was to say the very least filled with 'excitement'. He had left Maggie, left Jackie, and returned back to Maggie to find himself living at the bottom of the garden! Jet still treated Maggie on occasions with total disdain. For what it was worth he still believed that she loved him. Maggie allowed Jet into the house mainly for meals. Most of the time was spent among the empty beer cans strewn around the caravan. Work was now virtually non-existent. He was making Maggie and Norman's life a misery. He couldn't drive as he had no licence. He was now signing on and spending his giro down at the Basketmakers in Quedgeley. He grew steadily worse. Health was a major problem. Maggie recalls that there were some days when he just wouldn't emerge from the caravan, too drunk to stand up. It couldn't go on. It was about to come to a head.

Maggie wanted him out.

The children were beginning to loathe him. He wasn't much of a role model to them. Jackie had finally given up and for all Maggie's understanding she couldn't take anymore. She rang Norman Brodie.

Norman suggested that if he could get away for a few months it might the difference between life and death. He too had very few options. Jet had closed so many doors. Out of desperation he rang Mike. After speaking to his wife Linda, although it wasn't really practical as they only had a two bedroom cottage, decided to take him on to enable him to dry out yet again.

Maggie more than most knew how hard it was to take on such a hopeless case and didn't envy them one little bit. Driving up from Cornwall they arrived one Sunday morning sending Mike down to the caravan he knocked on the door. Jet didn't know who he was. His whole body was swilling with alcohol. Mike recalls the smell of the stale cigarettes and beer hitting him in the face. Jet told Mike to leave him alone for a while and closed the door. He didn't know what to do. Eventually Jet emerged from the caravan looking like death warmed up.

He was a shell of the man he was four months before.

Maggie, Norman, Mike and Linda sat at the table in the garden. Maggie had already warned them as to what to expect and within an hour they were on their way back to Cornwall. Jet insisted that he would do it his way and demanded that mike drop him off to pick up his 'breakfast' before the long trek back home... a six-pack.

The journey was to take a further five hours after another unscheduled stop for more ale in Taunton.

The cottage in Par came as a blessed relief. The journey had taken it out of Jet and on entering the cottage almost immediately fell asleep with his head resting on Linda's lap. Linda who was unaccustomed to such behaviour didn't know what to do. They managed to get him up the stairs and into bed. He slept heavily till the morning.

It was late September 1989.

For the first time in his life he was away from it all. He was away from the hassle most of it of his own making. He was determined not to let Mike and Linda down. Victoria, Mike's daughter was living away from home so her room became his for the next three months.

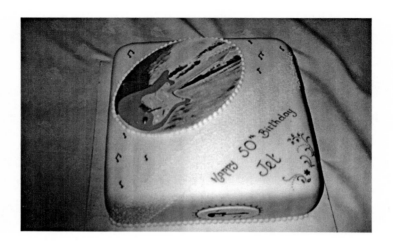

Jet's 50th Birthday.

DANCE OF THE PUPPETMASTER

Every morning for the past month had gone the same way. Maggie and Norman had done all they could to protect Jet from himself and from his children. It was a case of how the mighty have fallen. He only had himself to blame. He had slipped back into too many drunken stupors too quickly. The boys never said much; it had been the norm for so long they had begun to know nothing else. The previous six months he had totally isolated himself from them ignorant of their concern and their love.

Jet still had three gigs to do in November and without transport it was going to prove difficult. Mike was still working and until things improved financially, he had to run Jet around. Mike and Linda had taken a chance and he didn't want to let them down. He told them that he had to do it his way and not to interfere with his methods. Jonathan, Mike's son was still at home and they seemed to strike up quite a good relationship from the word go. The odd can or two used to disappear when they had the money. Jet for the moment had no money. He was totally reliant on Mike and Linda who never charged him anything for his keep. Mike took him along on the odd gig, guesting to earn his fag money for the week.

Mike and Linda knew that there would be many pitfalls along his road to recovery. Jet knew that however kind they were to him, they knew nothing about what it was like to be an alcoholic. Like many before, they seemed destined to fail.

Awaking that first morning was a little different. It wasn't like any other morning. The hustle and bustle of Gloucester had gone. It was so peaceful. Mike had offered to show him around the area. Within two minutes of leaving the cottage he was in sight of a pub. The rot had set in already.

Cyril and Mavis ran the Par Inn. Mavis had already had dealings with pop stars. Cliff and his entourage calling in for their pasties whenever they were appearing at the Coliseum. Their pasties were renowned all over the county. Jet insisted on going in without a penny in his pocket persuading Cyril to let him have a beer on tick until the following day.

It wasn't long before the locals were buying him drinks. He had that knack, and after all who was he to refuse such offers.Mike wasn't a big drinker but Jet always managed to persuade him to stay for a couple. Offering to settle the bill the next day was accepted. He never did. Mike had to pay it.

Jet always insisted that he would 'get it straight' himself. Without realising it within a week, he had already begun to use people. The first week found him in the pub virtually from opening time getting to know the regulars. Within a month he was returning home around midnight.Mike and Linda were helpless to do anything about it. The old habits were the same - the time and place the only difference. By Jet's standards he stayed reasonably sober still having no income, relying solely on the generosity of his hosts. He never went short of beer and cigarettes and the effort that he was supposed to be making from day one was as before disappearing down his neck. In all honesty he hadn't planned it that way, like a roller coaster it was gathering speed going downhill all the time. To supplement his drinking he would on occasions help out in the kitchen. Mavis baked amazing pasties. Cyril and Mavis were good to him. Mike offered to do a gig for them featuring Jet as a thank you for looking after him.

Mike and Linda were very patient. Rows were the norm after heavy bouts of drinking, sleeping it off overnight waking in the morning as if nothing had happened. Victoria's bedroom smelt like a brewery.

Jet had three gigs to complete in October. Dorchester, Derby and Torquay. Mike wasn't gigging that weekend and he and Linda offered to drive him to the venues. Tangent were appearing at The Buzz Inn, Dorchester featuring Jet a little later in the night. Arriving around six thirty in the evening bed and breakfast secured at a local hostelry they made their way to the gig. As always Jet invited a few fans back for a nightcap. Within the hour he was away with a young lady leaving Mike and Linda till the following morning. She had offered him back for'coffee' how could he refuse! Jet said that it was like jumping into bed with a woman who could have been his daughter! returning for breakfast the following morning as if nothing had happened. Linda couldn't believe it. Jet had been going on for weeks how he loved Maggie and how he was missing his boys saying he would give it all up for one more chance. He had had so many chances. It was a lottery. The tickets were free. No matter how many tickets he was given, he wasn't going to win the prize.

The gig at Derby found him performing alongside Mike Berry. The drive from Dorchester to Derby seemed to go on forever. Linda's parents lived in the village of Hilton about fifteen miles to the south of Derby. Having plenty of time a cup of tea seemed to be the order of the day. Mike knew a short cut and took the road through the tiny hamlet of Eggington. The car lost control and suddenly hit the kerb, the impact forcing the front wheel to buckle beneath the car. They managed to limp into the village and telephoned the venue with the news. The car was un-driveable, Jet began to panic. There was no problem getting to the job taking a taxi, getting back the next day wasn't going to be a long haul. Mike was in the AA and Cornwall was a long way away. The return journey from Derby was solved by one of Jet's most ardent fans who had travelled up from Leicester offered to squeeze them all in gear and all! to get them back to Hilton. Spending the night on the sofa in front of a coal fire eased his worries. Jet always worried, he had another gig on Monday at the Rainbow Hotel Torquay, and they all had to get there somehow.

Jet's usual breakfast, a can of beer and a fag followed on the Sunday. Mike contacted the AA and they were soon to be on their way. Whenever Jet was away he would on occasions ring Maggie to see if everything was OK. Mike rang. Norman answered. Mike's face dropped...

Panic was written all over Jet's face.

Replacing the telephone Mike set about explaining what had happened. A quick trip to the newsagents gave them the full extent as to what had happened. The front page of the News Of The World featured an exclusive on how Jet had left Jackie for Cliff's 'little sister!For Jet it was all too much. He left the room and headed for the back garden. He started to cry.

Jackie once again had twisted the knife. She had concocted a story about Jet and Donna. True they did meet up before his trip to Cornwall. True he did fancy her, he always had and probably always would, but this was something else!A few months earlier Jet and Donna had indeed spent time together. She had travelled up from her home in Willesdon to come and watch him at a local gig. Jet had even dedicated a tune to her Elvis's 'Love Me Tender' enjoying her company on the dance floor. Their meeting took place at Norman Brodie's house, in Elmore Lane.

Mike Longley a close friend and local radio DJ was also present. The business over, Donna and Jet returned to the Little Thatch a small hotel about a mile from Norman's home.Donna returned home the following morning promising to stay in touch.

Mike, Linda and Jet sat and discussed what had transpired and they all agreed that there was nothing that they could do until they returned home. The trip back took eleven hours. Reaching Lostwithiel around 10.15, Jet persuaded the driver to stop for fifteen minutes to enable them to get a quick beer in before closing time!Jet's entrance into the Kings Arms was announced with a head butting the wall. Mike and Linda had arranged to meet Pete and Helen Bevan that night believing that they would have all been back home long before that ungodly hour.

With only a short distance to go the cottage at Par was a blessed relief. The nightmare that had preceded was quickly forgotten. Mike's next-door neighbour Roy Trahar offered to drive them all to the gig at the Rainbow. Roy was a quiet unassuming sort of guy treating Jet as a normal human being. The arrival at the hotel was quite eventful. The Sun and The Mirror were there both looking for a story.

Tangent again did the honours sharing the bill with Don Partridge of 'Rosie' fame from the sixties. The show went well. Mike took control of the press even talking to the News Of The World on the telephone!

Prior to the trip to Derby a team of reporters armed with cameras etc. had 'encamped' themselves outside the cottage for three days! Norman R--------- Maggie's new man had answered the door back at Mafeking to three people who claimed to be old friends of Jet's. Norman whom Jet and Mike had christened Norman Normal was just a little naïve when it came to giving out addresses, especially with someone like Jet involved. He innocently told them of Jet's whereabouts and the ball was rolling. Jet was again in the limelight for all the wrong reasons.

Jet had always been hounded by the media. At one time he never seemed to be out of the press with some story or another appearing following him around like a bad penny. Mike's conversation with reporter Dan S----- at the Rainbow offered Jet the chance to respond to Jackie's allegations.

A meeting was arranged at the Carlyon Hotel St Austell. Judie M------ and two other reporters flew down from Manchester to conduct the interview. Jet for all his promises of reforming himself was still pretty much 'tanked' up. To give the impression that he was sober he drank nothing but orange juice that afternoon. Mike sat in, intervening when necessary, making sure that Jet didn't come out with anything that could be misconstrued.

A question suddenly appeared out of the blue.

'Could Cliff be the father of your son?'

It was obvious to Jet and Mike that all they wanted was to dig dirt on Cliff. For years the press have always looked for anything to hang on anybody. True Cliff did have an affair with Carol Jet's first wife but that was some thirty years before! Jet for all his 'waywardness' has always treated Ricky as his own son. Their paths very rarely crossed. They both lead very individual lives.

Jet to this day had always been baffled as to Jackie's motives. It could have only have been financial although Jet has always maintained that she did 'quite nicely' out of him during their time together. Jet never 'begrudged' her anything. Handling someone so volatile under the influence of alcohol takes some doing,

The proceeds of the story enabled Jet to purchase another car as well as to sort Mike and Linda out. They had stood out for nearly two months and Christmas was just around the corner. Jet was still unable to drive, his licence not being due for return until April 1990. The windfall from the story gave Jet fresh hope. He now had money to spend. He didn't want to give it all away behind the bar. He wanted to kick the beer into touch once and for all.

It lasted three days.

The sudden income and new found wealth saw Jet smoking upwards of seventy cigarettes a day. His health wasn't getting any better in fact he still hadn't made any inroads into giving up the alcohol. Accompanying Mike on his gigs gave him something to look forward to, although to be honest his playing was deteriorating rapidly. Mike was appearing at a pub close to the Tamar Bridge The Cornwalls Gate with Jet was making one of his 'guest' appearances. It was a total disaster. The excuse that he was mentally and physically tired didn't really wash with Mike. It was far from the truth. He was too drunk to hold a guitar. It didn't pass there. It was only three weeks since the Rainbow gig. Mike and Linda were taking so much from Jet that their patience was beginning to wear thin.

Mike had landed a gig at the Dartmouth Sailing Club. Linda, Jet and Jonathan set off in atrocious weather. The show went well and saying their goodbyes began the seventy-five mile trip back to Par. Jet for once had performed reasonably well. The journey was going well and it had stopped raining. About twenty-five miles out from Dartmouth midway between Morleigh and Diptford the car hit a large puddle in the middle of the road and just stopped. Mike and Jet got out to push it out of the water. It was coming up to one o'clock in the morning. Getting back in they decided to wait for about fifteen minutes to enable the car to dry out. Half an hour later it still wouldn't start. It had started to rain and by chance a passing car stopped and Mike and Jonathan were given a lift up to Diptford some three miles away to look for a phone box. Jet and Linda remained in the car. They were to remain there for over an hour both getting a little concerned as to the whereabouts of Mike and Jonathan. They were to return around three o'clock with the breakdown truck.

The patrol-man finally got them going and the relief of heading for home seemed to cheer them all up. The other side of Diptford disaster really struck.

This time it wasn't a puddle. It was a lake! The water was upwards of two and half feet and rising. Mike who had driven this way before stood no chance as the car ploughed into the swirling water. Nobody wanted to get out. The water was now in the car. The only saving grace was that the gear in the boot was raised another foot or so from the floor of the car. Mike had to get out and up to his thighs in water frantically tried to push the car. Despair and sheer angst set in. One by one they emerged from the car stepping somewhat uncertainly into the water. Mike had spotted the only light on in a farmhouse about fifty yards from the car and managed to summon them from their beds.

The folks who lived there couldn't believe what had happened. After drying out as best they could, the AA again was called. The patrolman couldn't believe it either...twice in one night. Jet had great concern as to how they were going to get the vehicle out of the water. With the equipment in the boot to tip it back by raising the car from the front would have proved disastrous, luckily they managed to extricate the vehicle with no water actually entering the boot. The time had now passed on to seven o'clock in the morning.

Sitting shivering in the rescue truck the immediate journey took them back to the main Exeter/ Plymouth road, where they were joined a little later by the main AA truck to transport them back home. They were to get another surprise. The driver was the same guy who had taken them all back about ten days before from Derby.. It was like saying hello to an old friend.

This was the ultimate nightmare.

The journey back to Par seemed like the regular thing to do. They reached the cottage at around ten that morning, some of the locals who knew the car looking on in amazement as they were yet again unloaded. The warmth of hot baths and the glow of the open fire together with coffee soon eased the horrendous events of the previous night. Mike was at the Par Inn that night. To Jet the beer never tasted sweeter!

The car took a couple of weeks to dry out. Mike's mate Ray from whom Jet had purchased the car offered to put it right. Again Jet was without transport. Mike's car was still off the road, so Roy again did the honours. Roy played a little bit of guitar and Jet sat in a couple of times playing Shadows tunes with him to show his appreciation for his help.

Christmas was weeks away. Jet had been at the cottage for over two months. He had good days and bad days. Mike was gigging at Looe Social Club overlooking the harbour. Being one of Mike's regular venues he had told them that Jet was coming along to do an impromptu spot.. the place was heaving. The word had got round that Jet was gong to make an appearance. The night went well Mike recalling that Jet played well apart from one incident. A couple were celebrating their wedding anniversary that night and were dancing on the floor.

Jet's mouth got the best of him yet again ordering them to move and get out of the way, he was playing and needed the space!Mike like so many other muso's Jet had worked with, covered up the embarrassment. What was turning out to be a good night ended when he demanded more drink at the end of the night. The bar had closed. Mike took the brunt of it yet again receiving another mouthful from Jet. This proved to be the final nail n the coffin. On the way home, an almighty row broke out in the car.

It was the drink talking. Jet thought he was king of the castle and totally indispensable. Mike couldn't take anymore. He finally snapped. Mike had invited two friends along that night and they couldn't believe what they were seeing and hearing, telling Jet that he was a has-been and that he didn't need this shit. Jet told Mike that he was going as soon as we returned to Par. Mike said fine and left it at that.

Mike was fuming. He and Linda had taken him in to try and help him and all they got was abuse. Mike had set aside around £800 in separate envelopes to cover Jet's debts back in Gloucester. He was determined to get them paid.

He showed him the door.

Andy one of Mike's friends who had been at the gig offered to put Jet up for the night. Andy too had had a drink problem and seemed not to be bothered by Jet's antics. He stormed out of the cottage, slamming the door behind him. He had money but nowhere to go.

The next few days were to prove crucial. It was December the 20th.

Once again the alcohol had taken over his life. he had abused hospitality on a big scale. The next few days were spent between Andy's cottage and the Cliff Hotel in Carlyon Bay. Jet had time to assess the damage that had been caused and hoped that Mike and Linda would have him back for Christmas. Jet returned to the cottage around one fifteen Boxing Day morning knocking on the door and stumbled in. Jet had been in a fight at another local, The Packhorse Inn in St Blazey Gate about a mile from the cottage. He had been flashing his money about and opening his mouth in all the wrong places, trying desperately to buy friendship.

Mike had just returned from a gig in Falmouth and both he and Linda were a little taken aback by his entrance as was Jonathan and his mate Leonard Pagett. Linda asked him what he wanted, Jet telling them that he was sorry and could he stay. The answer was no. Jet asked Jonathan for a cigarette. He had none. Jet apparently always had one for him when he was short but Jonathan insisted that he hadn't got any. Mike remembers that Jet really got nasty, swearing and throwing his weight around but it was all to no avail. Picking up his lighter, Mike threw it at him and handing him the money for his debts told him to piss off.

Jet had a gig in Gloucester the next day, Ray offering to drive him up. Jet was in no fit state to attempt the journey he slept rough that night. He had hit rock bottom.

The trip back to Gloucester wasn't the best. He wasn't looking forward to it but having to work that night at the Roundabout Hotel meant that he had to get himself together quickly. Booking in at the Little Thatch for bed and breakfast. Mike had informed Maggie that he was on his way up to see the children and had got some money for her, and Norman Brodie. Maggie enquired as to his mental state Mike telling her that he left under a bit of a black cloud one of the locals driving him up.

He never ventured once near Maggie and the kids. He never even sent them a card. The money went elsewhere. He managed to do the show and decided to ring Jackie in the hope that she might take him back. She agreed to meet him at the Gloucester Country Club eventually spending the rest of the festive season with her back in Matson. He had come up with a fair amount of money and knew that there was still a substantial amount left in the bank. Mike was in a bit of a quandary over it.

Mike knew where he would be. He rang Jackie. Getting no response he left a message regarding the money, informing her that he had spoken to Maggie and for the sake of the children would forward her the money. Jet had already run up a large amount of maintenance, and hadn't paid anything towards their upkeep for some time. Maggie had told Mike that they hadn't seen Terry(Jet) at all since his return.

Within a minute Jackie rang back. Jackie hit the roof. Mike was informed as to Jet's welfare telling him that he was 'drying' out in a clinic and that she and nobody else needed the money. Mike asked her for the address of the clinic so as he could settle the bill she refused to give it, fearing that Maggie would discover the truth. She knew that he was 'drying' out in the back bedroom at Jackie's house. Maggie told Mike to keep half of the money and send the rest to her. Linda and Mike had looked after him for three months and had had nothing in return but grief. Jackie had secured work during their separation. She was the only person left open to him. There was no love lost between Jackie and Maggie. To add insult to injury Jet was seen out shopping in Gloucester a few days later by his son. Jet totally ignored him.

Within a week Ray had returned Jet's car. He was saddened by what had happened and wished him well. Jackie now didn't want any part of the management side of the business and kept their relationship on a personal basis only. Alcohol was still rearing its ugly head. However hard he tried to beat it, it never left his side. It would be a further nine years before it did.

With little or no work on the horizon he continued his latest 'drying out' period. Jet did manage to do one gig for an old friend, Winkie Davies, a fan club member who had arranged a party and asked him if he would like to do a spot. Jet agreed. He was a bag of nerves. He hadn't performed in public for around two months.

The Architects provided the backing for the evening. Roland Humphries on bass, Baz O'Brien on drums, Roger Humphries lead, Mike Thompson sax and Dave 'Indigo Jones' Cremer on keyboards. It went well. The rest had done him good. Life back in Beauford Road too was becoming a lot easier. Jackie and Jet seemingly more relaxed, relaxed enough to purchase a couple of lovebirds, Chinese Quails.

It was May 1990.

Minehead followed by another gig at Brentford Football Club along with Don Lang and Terry Dene preceded a short break back in Holland, appearing again with the Arrows at Maassluis on the 15th June. The Rapiers were on hand to complete a gig at Camberley Civic Hall mid-month with Terry Dene and Tommy Bruce, completing the line-up.

Mardon House Farm. Devizes, found Jet back with Tangent who had replaced Roy Headford with Kevin Lang on rhythm guitar. The work was beginning to trickle in a little faster, the word once again was getting round.

Life with Jackie was once again becoming hard work. They tried desperately to get on. The time spent apart didn't do them any favours, Jackie coming along to the shows whenever her work enabled her to do so. A long weekend in Blackpool gave them the lift that Jet had needed. Three gigs helped to pay towards the Caravanette they had acquired with a little help from Jet's mum Winnie. Within four hours they were at Southport.

Phil and Dorothy Roberts had organised the weekend away. A couple of year had nearly passed since Jet's fiftieth birthday he was about to celebrate his fifty second working at the Gables Hotel. Pete Nelson who's band The Silhouettes provided the backing that night were superb with Jet receiving a cake baked by Phil's wife and presented by his two daughters.

The Silhouettes provided the backing for all three nights. The Moorcock Inn, Garstang filling the 8th July.

Jet and Jackie were a little apprehensive about the crowd at the Moorcroft; they were a little elderly to say the least. They both wondered if it was going to be one of those nights. It wasn't, and it turned out to be the best gig of the three. They couldn't wait to have them back! A radio interview preceded the final gig Phil driving Jet down to Radio Merseyside with Billy Butler and Wally Scott. The Lounge Bar at the Floral Hall Southport completed a highly successful weekend.

South Wales saw Jet take in three shows on the 12th, 13th, and 14th July. It was another chance to team up with Tangent at the Barrons Night Club, Swansea. Barry Memorial Hall, Barry the home of 'Winkie' Davies was the second port of call. Jet was pleased to see 'Winkie' although the show wasn't a sell out a fair crowd had turned up to see guest appearances from Mike Berry and Jess Conrad. who also took the stage. Jet and Jackie were both pleasantly surprised by the surprise visit of two old friends. Ulrich and Barbara Sasu from Aachen in Germany. They had spent some time with them during another trip on one of Jet's Dutch weekends in Rotterdam. They had both wanted to be there for his fifty first birthday but couldn't make it. They presented Jet with a belated birthday gift from their hometown - a beautifully decorated tin of biscuits and cakes! They were devoured with great pleasure!

The last gig at the Ely Festival at the Western Leisure Centre finished off anther great week. Marty Wilde topping the bill along with Johnny Preston. Johnny hit the top with his first single Running Bear (MercuryAMT1079) back in February 1960. it stayed in the charts for fourteen weeks. His follow up Cradle Of Love (MercuryAMT1092) climbed to number two in April of that year, staying in the charts for some sixteen weeks apart from a brief re-entry with Running Bear his last three recordings I'm Starting To Go Steady (MercuryAMT1104), Feel So Fine (MercuryAMT1112) and Charming Billy (MercuryAMT1114) never made any real impact although Feel So Fine did reach number eighteen in August staying around for ten weeks. Dave Sutch was also on the bill. Dave got Jet to do an unusual finale with him getting him on to sing on Chuck Berry's Johnnie Be Good. Jet's only other foray into vocals was way back in the sixties with Hully Gully and the old Everly's hit Love Is Strange.

It was back home to Gloucester for a well-earned rest. Jet still had serious doubts about his ongoing relationship with Jackie. It was blowing hot and cold. The next few weeks without any work were welcome but like so many times before he began to get tetchy. Apart from a show at the Worthing Assembly Rooms on the 24th with Mike, Tommy and The Searchers there wasn't anything on the horizon.

Dave Sutch rang Jet asking if he could fill in for him at The Futurist Theatre. Dave was recovering from surgery and didn't feel well enough to do the show. Tommy was there along with Heinz. Next stop, Cleethorpes, found Jet at the Beacholme Holiday Centre. It was a chance to try out yet another new band The Invitations. Jet remembered that they had to use them because the promoter hadn't paid the regular band their wages the previous night. Jet had struggled too to secure his wages on both nights. We shall just call him Bruce. After another night in the Caravanette Jackie and Jet returned home.

The year had gone so quickly. Cornwall was, or so it seemed, a long time gone virtually disappearing from his mind. The Orchard Theatre on the 6th September found Jet working with one of his favourite bands The Runaways. Jet had hoped to use them more after they had completed their '65 Special' tour. Phil Roberts had arranged another three gigs one back at the Moorcroft at Garstang, followed by one up in the Lake District at Kendal Town Hall ending back down in Southport for the final show.

Jet's fans have always remained loyal through the good and the bad days. The fan club boasts many members many of whom remained great friends with Jet, 'Winkie' Davies, John Robinson and Peter Jackson to name a few. The 30th September found Jet helping Peter out by playing for him and his wife on their wedding anniversary. It was the least he could do. Peter had followed Jet all over the country to catch as many gigs he could. Jet took his camera along to capture the moments. The night was totally informal.

October found Jet at the Assembly Rooms, Tunbridge Wells alongside The Fontanas and Mike Berry. Topping the bill that night were Marmalade. It had been a reasonable year for both Jet and Jackie with both of them seemingly more relaxed. Within months they were to part for good.

Hinckley Social Club towards the end of October he was up alongside Tangent. For Jet it was an easy night although no night is ever easy. It had been sometime since he had actually done any vocals, especially on record. Colin Pryce-Jones from The Rapiers had suggested that maybe they back him giving Jet the lead vocal on a new album that they were planning to release. Jet agreed to the track, maybe a Jet Harris vocal would be something different. The recording has been stored somewhere in the archives!

1990 was coming to a close. Dutch promoter Ton Verhagen had been discussing the possibility of another sixties show. Ton had asked Mike Berry to join Jet for the night and arranged to have '1961' a top Swedish band that both Jet and Mike liked provide the backing. Jet had worked with this outfit back in 1987 and couldn't wait for 1991 to arrive.

Life back in Beauford Road, Matson wasn't getting any easier. Jet began to spend more time with his birds than Jackie. He had acquired quite a collection making most of the cages himself. He had a makeshift aviary at the bottom of the garden, well actually it was a greenhouse full of plants and exotic birds! It took pride of place alongside Jackie's six dogs and six cats.. it was like living in a zoo!

Jet and Jackie had come full circle. The second time around didn't seem as good as the first. To the outside world all seemed well. She had dedicated herself to Jet Harris. Jet couldn't fault it. He felt like he was becoming a puppet, having to dance whenever she wanted to pull the strings. But this puppet didn't want to dance. Christmas was almost here. He had survived another year. One day he just got up and walked away. He didn't really care anymore. He wanted his freedom.

For the first time in his life he really did have nowhere to go. The friends at the bar had all disappeared. People, for good or bad didn't want to know. There was one option he hadn't considered...

He rang Winnie....

Bodmin Moor

Jet with Cliff Hall

Davey Graham and Jet Harris Con Club Shanklin

Mike, Wendy and Jet Yarmouth Isle of Wight

TWICE AROUND
THE HOUSES...

Christmas was spent quietly. Winnie hadn't planned on having an extra mouth to feed. For what it was worth he wanted to just become Terry Harris yet again. Leaving Jackie was the best thing he could have done. He suddenly found himself with time on his hands. The hullabaloo that had followed him throughout the previous year had truly drained the energy from him. The energy that remained had to be stored. It was time to stand back and take a good look at where his life had taken him and more important where it was going to take him from now on.

The relative safety of Winnie's little one bed-room bungalow in Upton St. Leonards about a mile and a half from the city centre was to serve him well. There were to be many more tricky roads ahead. Work at that time wasn't very forthcoming although after having a reasonable year before Jet really thought that it wouldn't pose any problem. Perhaps he had too much time on his hands... his reputation again found him wanting. Jackie had built his ego up and he was about to slip back into the depths of drink. Jet was well aware of the abuse he had put his body through especially over the last few years.

Winnie had always been aware of her son's problems. She was in her mid eighties and although very active and spritely for her age felt helpless. It had to be down to Jet. Nothing was too much trouble for her. Although he never intended to take her for granted, the odd occasion saw him taking advantage of her good nature

Winnie was leading a quiet life until Jet arrived. Jet for his part hadn't really spent a lot of time with his mum prior to that day, but would always do his best to shield her from any intrusions on his life. she was always pleased to see him although the thought of him returning to live with her didn't excite her, but being his mother she felt she had no choice, she had to be there.

Winnie was obviously very apprehensive and who wouldn't be, after all her son had been married and divorced three times! Jet promised to behave himself and that he would make a strenuous effort to reduce his ever-growing intake of beer. Winnie's main worry was the sleeping arrangements. The bungalow wasn't meant for mother and son.

Winnie gave up her bedroom. She slept on the sofa.... in the lounge.

Musically nothing was happening. It was as if he had disappeared from the scene altogether. The Event a few years earlier had promised so much, but like the numerous times before, drink had put paid to a lot of opportunities. His reputation was going before him.

The first few months with Winnie passed without any major setbacks. To Winnie it looked as if Jet had made the effort to reform by cutting down on his daily intake. Jet had no visible means of income, for the most part the Inland Revenue had seen to that. He was left with no alternative but to sign on the dole.

Signing on for Jet was nothing unusual. He had vowed never to do it again, but Winnie needed some visible signs of support and any money coming in would be useful. Winnie wanted Jet to get better. There would always be a can waiting for him every morning. Winnie would turn a 'blind eye' hoping against hope that it would see him through the day knowing full well that it wouldn't. The money he received from unemployment was in part given to Winnie, who in turn would give it back indirectly by buying him beer.

Jet rarely ventured out of the house. The Kings Head and the local store were the only places he would go. The landlord at the Kings knew about his problem. He was no different to the rest. He was there to sell beer. If Jet had the money he would take it.

The unemployment office was situated in the centre of Gloucester. To the girl behind the counter he was just another poor sod without work. A lot of people knew him and must have envied the position that he once had being so famous. Jet wasn't proud to be in this position, but this is what he had made. He had nobody else to blame but himself. To have the world at your feet only to see it washed away due to the poisoning of his body over the many years he had fought to regain his pride.

His respect had gone completely. He began to spend more and more time away from Win. He would spread out his dole money to cover his alcohol for the week. During this period he sold any remaining gear that he had to furnish his needs. Jet once bought a guitar for several hundred pounds only to sell it back the next week for half of what he had paid for it... to put it all down his neck or behind the bar...

Living with Winnie wasn't to be recommended. He had secured a bed-sit a stones throw from the Vauxhall pub. The room was damp and some of the windows were out.

The odd occasion he would return there if he were unable to find his way home. Winnie was the only woman in his life and although it wasn't perfect, her bedroom was far more welcoming than the damp one, at the back of the Vauxhall!

Life on the dole became routine. Sign on. The giro would arrive. Travel into Gloucester to cash it and head for the nearest pub. He always tried to put something aside for Winnie, yet on more than one occasion she got nothing. Jet said that he used to kid himself that he was drinking less, the reality was it was on the increase. It had been some time since he had attended Coney Hill. The clinic had already washed their hands of him and even if it were still available, he would have great difficulty in persuading them to take him back. Jet had tried on so many different occasions to shake the illness with it all falling on stony ground. The truth of the matter was that no one would treat him.

Winnie lived with the hope that one day her son would recover. Jet could turn in an instant and he did so on many occasions. Winnie didn't deserve it. When he eventually made an appearance after being 'out of it' all day his food would be waiting often refusing to eat it telling her that he would eat later. Winnie actually preferred him to be out of the house for fear of embarrassing her friends. Being an alcoholic couldn't have been much worse. Winnie knew all the tricks. She knew the score and worked around it for the sake of a peaceful life. The embarrassment of going to her local store to pick up her paper and coming out with a six pack of lager not to mention the cigarettes and rolling tobacco.

Jackie had become a distant memory. There were days when he would sit and ponder on what he had and might have had with her. Some days he thought of nothing else. When transport was available he would often ask them to drive down Beauford Road just to look. He had to let go. Bitterness remained. She had taken all that was left of him, his records, clothes and his guitars.

There was nothing left but memories.

Derek and Merv from Tangent joined him for one of his rare gigs at the Berkeley Arms, Cam near Dursley. Jet was really apprehensive about playing having not really touched a guitar seriously for a few months. Tangent ensured that he came away with his head held high.

Maggie and Jet still kept in touch, although somewhat like ships that pass in the night. When they were together they had a deep loving relationship. The bottle had indeed killed virtually all of that with Jet lying awake some nights when sleep wouldn't come thinking amidst the beer and haze of cigarette smoke. There was nothing in his life except his pint. Jet regretted deeply the way he let Maggie down. He would always let her down somewhere along the line, for she not only worked but had to raise a family as well. Jet was aware of the hardships and felt genuinely regretful for all the right reasons only for them to disappear as soon as he sat at the bar.

Winnie had never liked stardom. She was a very proud woman wanting like most mothers what was best for her son. She wanted Jet to be safe and happy. Being an only child herself she too was on her own. She had to cope with life and maintained that Jet should too.

The days seemed to rush away. There really seemed no way out. Jet did a bit of window cleaning helping an old drinking partner Trevor on good days. Trevor too was an accomplished musician and could knock out a mean tune on the violin. Trevor never really let on about his talent on the fiddle to the rest of the world he looked like an ordinary bloke. They would clean windows on sunny days and sit and drink on rainy ones! Either way, they would always end up in the pub!

Dave and Maggie Holbrook were still doing their best to keep the fan club going. With not much to say it was getting harder to fill the pages. With great sadness Dave decided to call it a day. The contribution that he and Dave Wheatley had managed to amass over the years for the newsletter seemed to be never ending. They could dig up snippets from everywhere. The last issue in June/July brought an end to an era. Jet still remained friends with them their warmth and love for him despite all his misgivings remained till the end.

Two years had passed since he had spoken to Mike Porterfield. Jet had happened to be in Molly Malones a pub in Barton Street when he noticed Mike's name on the board. Mike had steered well clear of Jet and had been living in Stroud. He still had the cottage in Cornwall but an enforced move away found him back in the area. Mike's name had began to pop up in quite a few pubs in and around Gloucester with Jet wanting to see him again if only for old times sake, but was pretty nervous at the prospect of doing so. Would Mike want to see him...

He decided to make contact.

They had shared many moments together. Jet needed a crutch. Mike had always inspired him when Jet wasn't on top form always having faith in him and never letting anyone put him down. Jet wanted desperately to get back in front of the general public. He needed to perform. They did have some good times together and felt that if he behaved himself and only drank in 'moderation' perhaps there might be a way back. Jet was still officially bankrupt and it would be nearer four years than three before he was free.

Mike had left his contact number with Norman Brodie. Agents of any standing do not give out other artiste's numbers. Jet was no exception. Norman refused to give it out. Jet wasn't one to be beaten. He rang Norman's assistant Clive Wilch inventing some cock and bull story of having mislaying Mike's number. A short discussion ended with Clive giving Jet the number. With his heart in his hands he rang Mike.

Mike agreed to meet up with Jet at the Prince Arthur a stones throw away from Molly Malones. Jet entered dead on opening time. He still had a major problem but decided to limit himself to one pint for the meeting. Mike was appearing at the pub the following Friday Jet asking if he could come along and play a couple of tunes for old times sake. Mike agreed and left it at that. As the week progressed Jet became more than edgy about the venture. Could he still play to any standard, after all he hadn't really done anything seriously in ages.

Only time would tell. Jet informed Mike that he hadn't got a guitar let alone any equipment for the gig. Mike told him not to worry, he would sort one out for him. Jet arrived at the pub looking like the Harris of old. He had a lot to prove that night and although he missed the occasional note his performance was greeted with warm appreciation from the regulars who had been looking forward to the night all that week.

Jet had got the buzz to play again.

Mike and his wife Linda had gone their separate ways. Wendy, Mike's new lady came along that night. Bob Phillips' a local agent had been actively involved in getting Mike plenty of work. Jet's reputation had followed him, only Norman Brodie coming up with the odd gig. Bob didn't want to take a chance on Jet who would tag along with Mike to his gigs doing a spot midway through the night. Jet's confidence began to gain momentum. Bob too was sitting up and taking notice and was toying with the idea of booking them out as a duo.

The first few months all went well. Jet was determined not to let this opportunity slip. He diligently tried to stay sober on the days that he was working. All of the gigs were Mike's, Jet getting the odd £10-£20 for his contribution. The money would always ensure that he could have a cigarette and a beer the next day.

Jet still enjoyed his pint at the end of the night. In Mike's eyes there was an improvement. It was all a façade. Jet had told Mike that he was giving Winnie the money from the gigs to help with her housekeeping. In reality he gave her nothing. True, he would hand over the money only to get it back the next day. The dustbin never seemed to contain anything other than empty cans!

Their reputation as a 'duo' began to spread. People wanted to see and hear more from Jet. Most landlords made him welcome wherever he went sometimes relying on Mike to get an extra few 'quid' to cover Jet's 'expenses!' Most of Mike's work took in the Forest of Dean. The Swan at Brierley gave Jet his first real thrill. Moray the landlord and his wife made Jet so welcome, hitting it off with the locals immediately. Paul and Sally Keightley two friends of Mike's lived in Ruardean about three miles from the pub, came along that night. Jet played out of his skin! Moray telling him that he would be welcome back any time. He would return some four months later.

Bob Phillips was putting the feelers out. The Jet Harris revival was under way again. Jet knew there was a long way to go and just playing kept his mind occupied. The money wasn't brilliant but in at least it was work. Wendy would come along some nights to keep him in check. She knew of his reputation long before she met Mike. She stood no nonsense.

John Welsh and his wife Pat also made Jet welcome. John and Pat ran The–Inn-On-The-Marsh at Moreton-In-The-Marsh. Mike took him along there one night being one of his regular gigs, the impromptu performance going down a storm. John invited them both back with their wives for dinner in the restaurant on the house. Mike had recently married Wendy and Jet had visions of taking Maggie along. He decided to take Winnie instead. The night coincided with her eightieth birthday. It was a lovely surprise for Winnie. She had earned it.

Mike and Jet continued to play at the pub a few times later. Jets performances were a bit hit and miss but he was always appreciated. The 'new' found fame and extra money meant that buying beer didn't pose a problem. It wasn't long before the drink began to have more than an effect on his playing. It was back in the old routine. He still hadn't got a guitar relying on borrowing one from Nathan, Mike's stepson. He had earned enough money to buy one but chose to drink it over the bar. The false image of being 'alright' on the night for the gig was harder to keep up. He was beginning to put it away in no uncertain terms. Mike and Wendy knew it and so did he.

Jet met up with Maggie on a couple of occasions during this period asking Mike if he could arrange the meetings! On one occasion Maggie ended up buying the drinks! Jet only having enough for one pint! She didn't seem to mind after all that was the Terry that she had come to recognise. Was there a chance of reconciliation?

Jet hoped so, only time would tell.

Mike had talked of returning to Cornwall. Work was pretty forthcoming so he decided to remain in the area for the time being. Jet had talked of setting up a studio after his bankruptcy was over to enable them to write and record without fear of any outside interests. Jet was still signed to Muff Murfin's organisation but as yet there were no immanent recording sessions in the pipeline.

Alec was still around and would come to see Jet whenever he could. Alec remembers one night at the

George Inn Newmarket near Nailsworth. Arriving en masse with a complete entourage along with Wendy and her residents (she worked in a care home) they filled the pub. There weren't many regulars in that night and those that were didn't really show any interest in the music. The night went well. Towards the end of the night the woman behind the bar asked Mike if they could liven it up a bit. Mike informed that he wasn't there to entertain the barmaids and continued to play. Without warning, Steve the landlord came from behind the bar and pulled the plugs from the wall. He told us that we had no right to insult his wife like that and informed Mike that no money would be forthcoming. Alec, Jet, Wendy and the twenty odd residents, had put a small fortune behind the bar. He told them to pack up and get out. Not only had they brought along the audience that night but he wanted free entertainment as well! Mike threatened to pull out all future acts unless he coughed up the cash.

The landlord was adamant. Wendy had already taken her party back to the home and trouble seemed to be brewing. Alec remembers that the landlord could have blown up a lot of expensive equipment with his stroppy attitude when he removed the power supply, and was ready to tackle any trouble head on.

Mike accepted the landlord's decision and started to dismantle the gear and loaded it into the car. The landlord who locals say was a failed footballer had some chip on his shoulder followed Mike into the car park. Mike reiterated his intent to stop all future acts staying completely calm whilst Steve argued with him.

Mike was refusing to be riled and Steve's voice began to get calmer. An apology to his wife would suffice. Mike reluctantly agreed and Steve agreed that that would be the end to it.

Jet and Alec ended up back at Mike and Wendy's place for coffee deciding to inform Bob about the fiasco that had ensued the following morning. Steve had already done that. Bob was furious. Mike insisted that it wasn't their fault. Bob had to do a free gig to compensate the landlord, the cheeky bastard still managed to get a free nights entertainment after all.

Autumn was fast approaching. Once again things between Jet and Mike were becoming strained. Jet was beginning to play less and less and drink more and more. Things really came to ahead when Jet complained to Wendy with regard to the guitar he was using. Wendy had bought it as a spare for Mike. Jet had been using it for some two months without any cost to him. He just added insult to injury.

One gig stood out from the rest. The Kings Head, Kingstanley. Jet had an absolute blinder. Mike knew he could do it. Even through the alcoholic aura that surrounded him it was only a matter of time. This was Jet Harris the superstar. Picking up nearly three times what he was used to ensured a good time the next day. How could it go wrong? It did, the very next day. Mike was appearing at the Churchdown Community Centre the following evening. Picking Jet up he sensed a slight 'change' but for then chose to ignore it. Jet had assured Mike that he was 'fit and able' to perform. Setting up the gear in the wrong part of the building they suddenly realised that they weren't supposed to be there. A couple of telephone calls later and yes he was appearing there only in the Social Club, which was attached to the main hall. Jet was gagging for a pint. having already drank a couple in the first twenty minutes! He was skint!

They were still in the wrong room when a couple of Mike and Wendy's friends Fran and Clive Holmes arrived with two of their friends. Anxious to catch up on all the gossip and introductions out of the way, Clive's friend offered to buy Jet a drink. Carrying on talking for a few seconds Jet interrupted to enquire about his pint. Telling him he would get it in a minute Jet's response was dreadful.

'You'll f---ing go up and get it now! So f—king hurry up'

Wendy and Fran who heard it were furious. They had every right to be. Jet didn't even know these people luckily for Jet, Mike didn't hear what was said, if he had he would have hit the roof.

He didn't get his beer.

Jet had blown some thirty-five pounds on drink that day his previous pick up from the night before. He even had the nerve to ask Clive if he could borrow some money to get himself a beer. Clive refused.

When the gig finally got underway it was close on ten fifteen. Jet sat there with a face like a smacked arse. He wanted to play. Everybody knew that he was totally incapable of doing so. He turned to Wendy and said

'He ain't gonna let me play tonight is he?'

'No' came the reply. 'you're drunk and incapable.

Jet's first thought was there goes my beer money for the next day. He demanded to be taken home immediately. Wendy offered to drive him straight away and frog marched him out of the building. She pulled no punches laying it on the line that his vile and abusive attitude wouldn't wash. Jet realised he had overstepped the mark. He 'sobered' up in an instant. And went back in and sat down. He started to cry.

It was the beginning of the end. A few days later, a gig at the Home from Home on the outskirts of Cirencester also ended in disaster. Mike and Marilyn Pugh who also ran a restaurant in the town had booked Mike and Jet to appear, having already being introduced to Jet at the restaurant by Mike. Mike was expecting a full house having advertised the gig both on radio and TV, and even managed to get it mentioned in the National Press. The place was packed. Jet was totally obnoxious making a complete fool of himself. It was left up to Mike to carry the night. It was July 1993. The latest comeback had again began to run out of steam.

A gig at Forest Green Rovers Football Club, Nailsworth proved yet another nail in the coffin. It was Mike's gig and Jet tagged along looking for a spot to pick up some money for the next day. Mike always tried his best to get a little extra on top of his fee to help Jet out. Jet took it as the norm, expecting to get paid regardless of how good or bad he was that night. That night he was atrocious. On the way home he asked for his pennies asking Mike how he had performed that night.

Mike would always praise him when he did well and Jet had to learn to accept any criticism from time to time. It was an important gig for Mike that night. Jet didn't enhance his or Mike's reputation that night, who unbeknown to Jet was beginning to lose work because of Jet's incompetence and sometimes downright rudeness.

Mike told Jet that he was awful. Jet replying,

'I'm Jet Harris and I earn more than you in one night than you do in a week!'

His mouth just rolled on. The reality was that he hadn't actually done a memorable solo gig for eighteen months!

Mike stopped the car and ordered him out. Jet got out and slammed the door behind him. It was one o'clock in the morning and he was seven miles from home. He managed to take a taxi. The following week he never said a word when Mike called round to pick him up for the next gig.

The embarrassing moments were coming almost nightly. Jet just didn't realise what he was doing. Having met a young lady at a gig a few weeks before at Newbury he invited her over to the gig that night. Pat and her family turned up at Thatcham Football Club looking forward to the evening. Newbury being some fifty miles from Upton, and with no transport courting was going to prove a bit of a problem. That night there was no end to his stupidity. The look on her mothers face as he announced from the stage that his future mother-in-law was sitting in the audience! What a prat! That wasn't the end of it; he couldn't afford to buy her a drink ending up scrounging from the other guests around the room!

Needless to say… they never got married!

Chepstow British Legion went the same way, the alcohol seeing to that. Having played a couple of tunes in the first spot retired to the downstairs bar for a couple of beers, during the break. Jet amidst the backslapping managed to down four pints in twenty minutes, telling a woman in her sixties to shut the f—k up and listen to the music! The alcohol had rendered him incapable of playing yet again. Mike and Wendy were furious. Nobody spoke on the way home. Jet was too far out to even notice.

Mike never went back again.

The biggest gig of the year came at the Rock For The Forest at Cinderford. Jet was billed as the main attraction and having done his bit on local radio promoting the show was looking forward to the night. Taking the stage with Mike proved again that all was not well. The sound was awful. Making a swift exit wasn't easy. The most embarrassing moment of the evening came prior to the show when entering the building wasn't recognised by the woman on the door, telling him that the Green Room was for Artistes Only!

The reviews were awful. They were the worst performers on. It was a charity show and to top it all, Jet demanded some money from the organisers for his performance!

Jet was to play his last gig with Mike on their return to The Swan, Brierley. The promises he made to Mike and Wendy to stick with orange juice were to prove hollow that night. Wendy said,

'Orange Terry?' He just grimaced replying,

'I want a pint!'

The nights were getting very few and far between when he was able to afford many drinks, relying on the generosity of others. There was never any shortage of folk wanting to buy him a glass of ale. Winnie knew the score, always being fast asleep when he returned late at night. Being Jet Harris, people wanted to be around you. Having already consumed his daily 'safe' quota by three o'clock that afternoon the session to come that night was a bonus.

Mike had previously tuned the guitars up ready for his first spot. When Jet joined him the guitar immediately went straight out of tune! Mike did another song and Jet retuned the guitar and giving Mike the nod started again. Immediately a string snapped. The beer kicked in and he started to get angry, snatching the guitar from around his neck. He demanded to know where the strings were, Mike's strings! By this time he really was seeing red. Trying to remove the broken string he managed to snap another! Throwing the guitar down knocking an ashtray from a table, he made his way back to where Wendy was sitting.

Jet really couldn't see how to put a string on he was so pissed. A fan that had come along especially to see him offered to help put them on for him. He seemed to feel honoured to help. The guy managed to get the strings on for him when he immediately snatched it back from him, telling him he hadn't got a bloody clue. Wendy told Mike that the guy was close to tears. It was so sad.

Jet's insistence brought the final straw, his attempt at tuning broke a third string! Something told him he wasn't going to play. In desperation he tried to get the strings into some sort of order staggering towards Mike who threw his guitar lead at him and plugged him back in. the sound was bloody terrible. That was it. Mike told him to sit down and not to bother. Once again the beer money had gone for next day. He continued to shout insults at Mike. Wendy who had become more reluctant to come out on the gigs grabbed him by the arm. Not another word left his lips. Beer or no beer he knew he had blown it, trying to laugh it off a short time later with folks at the bar. The damage this time had well and truly been done. It was over.

Sleep that night didn't come easy. Another bite at the eternal cherry. Jet never stopped once to think of what he had thrown away. People from all walks of life had sponsored his lifestyle for to long. Mike and Wendy covering expenses all the time. He was always moaning about something. He begged Mike not to tell Winnie how bad his behaviour was. He couldn't help it. It was all down to alcohol.

Winnie never cottoned on that all was not well between Mike and Terry. They never played together again. About three weeks later the phone rang. It was Mike.

It had been a couple of years or so since Dan S----- had been in touch. Dan had informed Mike that he needed to interview Jet about a publication that was in the pipeline for possible publication. Having already spoken to Tony Meehan and Carol Costa Jet's first wife from the late fifties he just needed confirmation of what they had said. Jet began to smell a rat. Winnie still had visions of the press knocking on her door. For all Jet's faults, he didn't want it either. Mike assured them both that the press would not be coming round. There was nothing to it. He agreed to meet Dan.

Mike picked him up and they drove to Bath for the meeting with Dan who was arriving on the six o'clock train. Dan who lived in Henley on Thames didn't bank on what was about to happen that night. Over a drink in a local pub the meeting got underway. Jet looked to Mike for guidance something he had done in the past. It wasn't forthcoming; Mike knew nothing of the content of the interview. The whole thing should have been done and dusted in about forty-five minutes. Jet had other ideas. There remained still a little arrogance with Jet continuing to demand drinks, before considering what Dan had to say. A cheque for £2000 was on the table for confirmation of what he wanted to know. To offer that sort of cash it had to be something big.

Jet still refused to give any answers either way. Dan had arranged to catch the nine o'clock train, the last one that night back to Henley. Through Jet's stubbornness he missed it. Dan asked Mike if he could run him home offering to pay for the petrol. Mike agreed.

It was one o'clock before they reached Dan's home. Still demanding drink and fags, Jet kept evading the questions until two thirty that morning, finally confirming the others story. Jet and Mike arrived back in Gloucester around four thirty that morning. they had been out of the house twelve hours! Dan arranged to complete the deal the following week the day before Mike had had to go to Weymouth on business. Jet had been trying to contact him all day, leaving numerous messages on his answer machine. Mike had driven back through torrential weather and immediately rang Jet.

Jet let fly, telling Mike that under no circumstances was he going to sign any contracts with Dan, he didn't want the money. Mid conversation he pulled the phone from the wall. Within twenty-five minutes Mike was knocking on Winnie's door. He didn't mince his words. Jet told him in no uncertain terms that he was adamant and had no intentions of completing the deal. He told Mike to f—k off in front of Winnie. Mike reassured Winnie that there was absolutely nothing to worry about, Dan if he wanted, could proceed with it with or without Jet. He started to mouth off violently.

Mike replied, 'Your not with one of your fans now Terry, Winnie, you don't know the half of it'

Jet responded telling Mike to 'f—k off out of it then'

Mike left. The story never came out.

Winnie couldn't believe what she had just witnessed. Mike knew of Jet's apprehension rightly so, having had many altercations with the media over the years. Winnie had her share of cameras and reporters. They didn't speak much about the outburst. Mike and Winnie both knew it was the cry of a frightened man. It was time to do what Wendy had suggested some time earlier... time to stand back and take a good hard look at what he was, and what he had become. He didn't like what he saw.

He hid his fears once more behind the bottle.

Within weeks Mike and Wendy returned to the cottage in Cornwall. It would be another two years before their paths were to cross again. Christmas was there yet again. Jet decided to make a play for Maggie. For some time he had kept the thought in his head that maybe there could be reconciliation. He needed another crutch to lean on. Maggie had in fact considered taking him back, but always shied away when push came to shove. Her senses always came around at the right time.

Christmas again like the previous year was spent quietly with Winnie. Jet sat waiting for a call from Maggie hoping that she would have him over to see the boys. The call never came. He called them and wished them

Merry Christmas wishing them all well. He took Winnie down to the Kings Head for a Christmas drink, trying hard to keep his dignity. Everybody wants to buy you drinks at Christmas but on this occasion, he refused. A couple of pints were just enough. Returning home eating their festive dinner they both fell asleep.

Soon it would be nineteen ninety four...

Winnie

Jan, Glovers Cottage Peacock Hill

PEACOCK HILL.....

Christmas passed. Jet and Winnie seeing the New Year in quietly. What would that new year bring? Jet felt that he had indeed reached rock bottom. Three years full of so much hope filled with so much sadness and despair. The bar had never been far away. Winnie had always given it her best shot and although at times she could be a little cantankerous, he would have been lost without her. She was the last refuge from the storm. For the moment he was safe.

Jet virtually had only the clothes that he stood up in. It was bus fare only travelling into town, going through the ritual of signing on. Dole money one day gone the next at either the Vauxhall or Molly Malones. Trevor his old window cleaning 'partner' would see him alright any time he was short, which was most of the time. They had an arrangement whereby they would lend each other a fiver till next giro day, their monies coming through in opposite weeks meant that they would always have enough for a couple of pints!

Molly Malones' held good memories. Jet and Mike used to run a jam session there every Monday evening. Muso's from all over Gloucester would roll up to play for a pint of beer. Mike and Carol O'Connell ran the pub and as the name suggests, it was frequented by more than its fair share of Irishmen! Those days were over. Wherever his music had taken him it always ended up back in some bar or other reflecting on what might have been. He seemed to fill his days sitting in the pub. His will to survive was at an all time low. The musicians who played the pubs and clubs in and around the city would often ask him to get up and give them a tune, knowing full well that he wasn't really able to do so. They just wanted to take the piss. People were laughing at him. Although he was at rock bottom he had one thing over all of them...

He had been there, he had reached the top, and they never would.

Jet for the most part enjoyed being Jet Harris. Being just plain Terry especially after all the ups and downs he had endured would have been nice, but having put himself up so many times only to be knocked down, meant that he would only reap what he had sown. Being pleasant came easy especially if there was a drink at the end of it. It was if he was proud of being seen drinking, and had to live up to the reputation that he had made for himself. Week after week he would continue to kid himself that he was in control. Those who had any sense saw straight through it. You cannot control alcohol... it controls you. Being who he was he honestly believed that people wanted to rub shoulders with him. It gave him a buzz, always ending up abusing their friendship and hospitality.

Alcohol made him treat people like shit.

Many people deal with trauma in different ways. Jet recalled Maggie losing her uncle suddenly. He didn't ask to die. He was just a normal bloke. Having had a couple of close shaves with death himself Maggie said it should have been him. Looking back Maggie was probably right; yes it should have been him. Alcohol serves up so much selfishness and disregard for other people's feelings, and he knew all about that. He had been left clinging to the hope they maybe one-day people would understand. With Maggie he had smashed all they she had put before him.

Alcohol is full of excuses, that's all there is. Any excuse to go down to the pub. Maggie said that when someone takes on an alcoholic, it's going to be an uphill struggle. Firstly, you take them on for who they are, secondly, because you believe that underneath it all, there is a nice guy trying desperately to break free, and thirdly because you honestly believe that you can sort out their problem. Jet didn't look for sympathy. He knew then what he had lost. His boys Ben, Sam and Craig were growing ever more distant from him. True he would visit them sometimes, but life had to go on. His saving grace through it all was that Maggie was always there albeit standing in the shadows. In her own way she still is.

Jet made many mistakes in his life. The last one for the road always breaking the camels back. If it were there, he would have it, having to face the consequences and all the trauma that it would bring. The last few years had made him very self-centred to the extent of not being served due to his rudeness. Perhaps it was too late to change... having lived with this constant need for alcohol.

For now his time centred around the Kings Head and The Vauxhall a drinkers spit and sawdust pub. The locals used to protect him, feeling safe from the media, but would desert him when the money ran out... the bar was the only place he felt safe. The day Jet's bankruptcy ended he breathed a sigh of relief. The last four years had seen the courts taking most of his royalties to pay off the debts. Suddenly he didn't have to go looking for someone to buy him a beer. Jet, who had always been generous with money when he had it, was now in a position to afford a lot more with the comfort of the royalty cheque.

Jet contacted Maggie to tell her the good news, giving her a couple of hundred pounds to help her out. It didn't seem a lot, and it couldn't make up for all the hurt he had put her and the children through. Winnie became the proud owner of a new washing machine, it was the least he could do. His visits to the Vauxhall were getting less. He was spending most of his time and money down at the Kings.

Through all of it he never lost sight of what he had had and what he could have had. He lived with the belief that he could still do it and that one day he would again prove them all wrong. An opportunity came to perform at a charity concert in Gloucester. It was November 1994. It was the chance he had been waiting for. Perhaps he could silence his critics once and for all. Jimmy Sloane and Lee Sharp from Cheltenham were the only two guys with whom Jet had played fleetingly, mainly at Lee's pub in the town. Purchasing another guitar he set about practising his set. Jet always suffered with stage fright. That night was to be no exception. Having his usual two pints of 'Dutch courage' before making his entrance he tried to steady his nerves. There were a lot of people out there who for the most part were all pleased to see him. He didn't want to let them down.

It turned into a fiasco.

From the moment he set foot on stage, everything that could go wrong did go wrong. He had decided that his own guitar wasn't good enough and neither were the others. He had plenty to choose from, but just panicked. He got frightened and stormed off the stage, finding solace back at Wins' with a couple of cans of lager.

Jet had stood back and looked before. This really was the point of no return. People had told him he was still lucky to be there. Alcohol had cocooned and surrounded him for nearly thirty-five years. Could he escape? Would the real Jet Harris ever shine through? Perhaps he already had. Since his time with Maggie, he had always been looking for the Mrs Right, someone to give him that love and understanding that he longed for. Maggie had given him that, but now she wasn't there. It was now up to him. The journey looking for that light at the end of the tunnel had seemed to go on forever. Something told him that all would be revealed in the fullness of time.

Something had to change...

Apart from Jimmy and Lee, musically Jet had felt like throwing the towel in. One day the phone rang. Brian Ashby a life long friend and avid fan of Shadows music told him that Hank was appearing in a show in Bournemouth and would he like to go. Feeling a little reluctant at first, he thought the trip away might do him some good.

Jet and Brian had been to a couple of shows together in the past. Brian picked him up and on reaching Bournemouth booked into the Truville Hotel. It was November 1995. Hank was appearing at the International Conference Centre. Brian and Jet arrived at the centre mid afternoon and headed for the bar. There were two young ladies working there, one of them thought she knew Jet's face. She came over to where they were sitting and introduced herself. Jet apparently, had always been her childhood hero. It transpired that it was her birthday and Jet gave her a fiver wishing her all the best, asking her if she would be there for the show later that night. She told them that she had to come back to conduct a stock take but they might not see her. They said goodbye and headed back to the hotel. The young lady's name was Janet Fletcher.

Brian, who had to do some business later that afternoon, left Jet in the safety of a local pub for a couple of hours. Jet only drank one pint all afternoon. Bishop's Tipple isn't the weakest of beers, and he didn't want to let Brian down by rolling out of the door drunk. Returning to the hotel to wash and change, they made their way back to the Centre for the show. A short while into the performance Jet decided that he needed a drink. Secretly he was hoping to see Janet again, and to his surprise she appeared and sat down beside him at the bar. She had wanted to see him again and had been hoping that he might feel the same.

Jan was the Senior Service Supervisor at the Centre. They got talking and it transpired that she used to have Jet's photo on her bedroom wall when she was only four years old! They seemed to hit it off immediately and exchanged telephone numbers, Jet promising to call her in a couple of days. True to his word he did and invited her up for a weekend. Changing her rotas' she made her way up to Gloucester. Jan was different. She wanted to call him Terry not Jet. Making his way to the bus station, he sat waiting with his overnight bag for her to arrive. They booked into the New Inn a fourteenth century hotel in Gloucester. It was nigh on the middle of winter and with the radiators 'up the shoot' still managed to sleep with the windows open all night!

She was no sooner there than she had gone. There were tears all round. Jet had really enjoyed her company and didn't really want her to leave. Brian had noticed the 'magic' between them. Jet couldn't wait to see her again. He didn't have to wait long. One phone call was all it took. Within a couple of weeks, Jan had given in her notice and was on her way to Gloucester. She knew his situation wasn't in the best of shape, but felt that it was where she wanted to be. She wanted Terry, not Jet for who he was.

Winnie was ecstatic. Janet and Jet set up home on the 25th January 1996. She was the best thing to happen to him in years. He was still enjoying his beer, but he was beginning to change. She was to play a major role on his road to recovery. Jet didn't want to lose this woman. He began to make a steadfast effort to beat the bottle. Jet had managed to cut his daily intake down to just three pints a day. Jan who enjoyed a drink occasionally stopped completely. He didn't want to risk losing her.

He followed suit.

Being an alcoholic for so long meant being tough on ones self. He was determined to beat it. It was as if the stupor that had followed him around for so long had started to evaporate. It was hard but it was getting easier every day. He began to get the urge to play, wisely investing some of his money into two new guitars. Jan had given him purpose, he was going to grasp it with both hands. He wasn't gong to let her down.

Jan managed to secure work behind the bar at the Kings' Jet's local in Upton. On occasions, he would sometimes serve from the other side of the bar! The regulars couldn't believe it. The past was the past. He couldn't change what had happened. The future he could. He was now in control of his own destiny. Although it was still early days, waking up without the need for a few cans of lager was a blessed relief.

Jan continued to build a new life with Terry. She knew that there was a long way to go before he had put enough breathing space between him and his demons. Jet stuck to his task and both he and Jan were to find themselves flying off for a holiday. Brian and another friend, Barry Gibson had been in touch with the owner of a castle, Amaedeo Maffie. Amaedeo had always been a great fan of the Shadows, and was more than happy to have them both over. He knew Jet was on the road to 'recovery', and offered the use of his therapy room to both of them to aid the process. The treatment was to prove very beneficial. Lying on a couch, electrodes were attached to their heads, which in turn were fed to a TV monitor. The therapy reduced the heart rate and the craving for drink seemed to vanish. The beauty of this place was that there were no televisions, no papers, no radio, just pure total relaxation. Jet and Jan were the only two people in the castle!

The outlook on life had changed completely. Amaedeo had promised that the treatment would make them both look and feel a lot better. Jet wanted to be weighed. Marco one of the assistants took him to the scales. Though its all kilos these days, he always wanted to know his weight in pounds. Marco had this lovely way of calling them LUPS!. During the stay they were both given their own doctor, nurse and two maids who would to attend to their every need. The warmth and hospitality was unsurpassed.

The Sunday meal was something else. The staff who seemed to live in a commune all cooked something different and brought it along to a grand dining room within the castle, to be shared amongst everyone. The trip to Italy had really given Jet a boost. There was no medication. All his nerves seemed to have disappeared, and apart from a few aches and pains in his ankles, it felt like all the badness was leaving his body. Apart from the Sunday special Jet and Jan were given a list of the foods that they could eat. His cholesterol levels had doubled, and needed to be addressed. Chiara, Amaedeo's wife wished them both good health, telling Jet that he had a good few years left in him yet!.... he felt like a new man.

The return to the reality of cold dank Gloucester didn't deter them. His visits to the pub had now taken the right turn. It didn't include alcohol, he even had his photo taken once drinking tea!! Jan suddenly developed a problem with her left foot and although not major, returned to Bournemouth to get it attended to. The waiting time in Gloucester was too long. During the stay in Bournemouth Jet received a telephone call from a dear old friend and muso, Laurel Jones. Laurel asked Jet if he would like to perform at Lee Sharp's new club in Cheltenham. Telling Laurel he would sleep on it, on their return both he and Laurel went over to see Lee. Geoff O'Brien another mate of Laurels' made up the threesome. Geoff played rhythm guitar. They were all a little 'rusty' to say the least, but decided to give it a go. Advertising for a drummer soon found Richard Browning who also played keyboards. Rehearsals got underway.

Their first gig took in the Hospital Club at Cheltenham. There was no money involved; playing for charity they took the place by storm. Jet had given so many people so many reasons to doubt his ability over the years that he had even began to doubt his ability himself! He performed to the highest standard. He was on the way back. The band was beginning to get noticed. Dave Carson, and ex DJ from Radio Luxembourg had shown an interest, and fancied taking them on under management. They would have to wait and see.

Jet had been dry for many months decided that it was now safe for him to apply for his driving licence. There was a time limit in which to apply and it seemed a sensible option. Because of his previous 'form' he was required to take a medical. The blood test proved negative and much to his relief his licence was returned.

The boys did the odd gig at Lee's club. During one of these gigs Jet and Jan were to meet up indirectly with Billie Davies his old girlfriend from the sixties. Billie had apparently left her music at the club one night. It was an excuse to visit her and return her dots. Walking into Billies' Jet burst into the Searchers 'When You Walk In The Room' which was very apt at the time!

Jan got on great with Billie. Billie will always hold a special place in Jet's heart, for it was she who pulled him out of the car all those years ago in Worcester. They talked of a possible sixties show and on their return Jet rang Dave to see if he could do anything. Dave immediately got to work and arranged a gig in Swanage, with Billie coming along as a guest. The show went well.

Jet and Jan had now been together for almost a year. They loved each other's company, but more importantly loved and cared for each other. They decided to get married and on the 23rd December at Gloucester Registry Office, they tied the knot. This was to be Jet's fourth marriage. Mike and Wendy came up from Cornwall, Mike having the honour of giving Jan away. He had noticed the difference - Jet was a different person. Dave Holbrook and Dave Wheatley also took time out to attend.

Having come so far he wasn't going to let it slip now.

The accommodation in Western Road wasn't the best. A move to a small bedsit in Upton St Leonards found them living over a detached garage. Though only small, it was warm, cosy and most of all, dry! Jet still enjoyed his alcohol but the time was drawing ever closer for his need to break free from the restraints that it had imposed on his life. Janet was a new beginning. He didn't want to risk losing her.

The year was to be tinged with sadness. Already having lost Sam Curtis Jet was about to lose another close associate, Jerry Lordan. To Hank, Bruce Tony and Brian, he was more than just a friend; he amongst others contributed so much to more to instrumental music than any other in the history of British pop music. Jerry was a legend amongst legends. 'Apache' apart, he was responsible for many of the Shadows finest moments. 'Atlantis', 'Wonderful Land' and for Tony and Jet, their number one 'Diamonds'. He also wrote the follow up that reached number two, 'Scarlet O'Hara'

His funeral was attended by many show business personalities. For Jet it was nice to catch up with Tony and Bruce again. The circumstances were a little harrowing but they talked of old times and shared their memories of Jerry. Alec still talks warmly of the man who he knew as a friend. 'Apache' seems such a long time ago, and it is a tribute to his stature that his music is still being performed to day. Jerry left a legacy of wonderful tunes that have stood the test of time. Genius is hard to replace and for Jet it was a pleasure to have known him.

Jet and Jan were to move yet again, to a flat in Southgate Road in the city centre. It was handy for all the pubs! Which Jet was still frequenting. Jan said they were endless days, finding themselves in and out of the local hostelries, Jet once again sleeping only to wake again to do the same thing the following day. Although his drinking had eased it was still causing Jan a bit of a problem. She began to wonder what she had let herself in for. They didn't fancy living in the city centre and a move to Cam, near Dursley, about eight miles to the west of Gloucester found them occupying a flat. It was a far cry from the hustle and bustle of town life, and Jet's choice of drinking establishments dropped dramatically. They were happy for a while but there had to be better times around the corner. The flat in Draycott Avenue wasn't up to much but offered slightly more room than their previous accommodation in the city centre. They were to remain there until December 1999.

Musically Jet wasn't really going anywhere, doing the odd pub gig to pay for his beer and help towards the rent. Life was becoming routine, there had to be a way out. They both had something in common sharing an affinity for the Isle of Wight, Jet from his childhood days, and Jan having lived on the island with her first husband. Jet had always believed that he was 'conceived' there and it seemed like a good excuse to visit Jan's daughter Kim who lived in Ryde, and anyway, the break would do them good.

The visit did the trick. They both agreed that this was where they wanted to be. Their time in Gloucester had virtually run its course. There was nothing there for them. From his time in Cornwall Jet had always wanted to live by the sea. They returned home full of anticipation and expectation, packing almost immediately. Jet still had one gig to complete at the Kings Head, in Dursley. Alec his trusted friend who had been with him through thick and thin offered his assistance. He above all others had earned the right to be there on Jet's last mainland gig for the next few years. Loading the gear into the car at the end of the night felt like the end of an era for him. Little did he know at that time, that he and his new wife Jill would also follow in Jet and Janet's footsteps and settle in Sandown.

The move to the Isle of Wight came at the end of 1999. Jet and Janet said goodbye to Cam and headed for Portsmouth. The frost lay heavy on the ground as they waved goodbye to Gloucester. For Jet the city had given him hope and much more despair as his time there had gone on. It was just a downward spiral. The move to the island was to be the best move of his life. They secured bed and breakfast for a few weeks before finally finding a cottage to rent on the outskirts of Bembridge. Winnie too would find herself moving to Cowes within eighteen months. The mass exodus from the mainland continued when Alec and his wife Jill moved over four years later. Mike and Wendy too were to move over to Sandown in 2005..

A grade two listed cottage tucked away from the madding crowd, about two miles out of Bembridge was to be their home. Gone were the days of Barton Street and all the shit and endless drag that life had thrown his way. As a child he had always felt that he might return to the island but some fifty years on, it should have come quicker! But he was there now and that was all that mattered. Jet and Jan set about building a new life together. Jet threw himself into constructing a garden. There wasn't a can in sight! Turning his back on the mainland, spending time relaxing in this new secluded part of his life. The work would take him many years but the end product would be worth it.

The pace of life on the island was similar to that of his time in Cornwall. Being so laid back it took time to adjust to the life of a country gent! To be able to walk along the beach whenever without fear of the press hounding him, without the fear of needing to find a pub. True he still went into pubs whenever he could. Old habits die hard, but to his determination and credit he only drank tea or tonic water! Behind every man is a good woman. Jan kept him on the straight and narrow, together with Maggie they were the only two who had any chance of doing anything for him. He had let so many people down so many times before. The isolation of the cottage gave him time and space to breath. Although Jan was behind him, it was Jet who wanted to stay 'dry'; he and he alone did it. There would be no holding back. He still had so much to give and so much more to achieve.

He gave up drinking.

The year was 2000.

Jet and Jan had established themselves safely on the island, Jan finding work at the Windmill, a hotel in Bembridge. John Hannam, a local presenter on Isle of Wight radio invited Jet along to the studio to do a couple of interviews. Vic Farrow a friend of John's asked if he could come along to the studio to meet Jet. Sitting outside the studio they got talking and inevitably the conversation got around to music. Jet talked of the possibility of doing a couple of shows on the island. Vic had connections in the business and offered to put a show on for him. Within three months Jet found himself appearing with Mike Berry, The Rapiers and Cliff Hall at the Medina theatre on the island on the 11th June. A second show was to follow featuring John Leyton also at the Medina. The show went down well, Vic deciding to take the same format to Babbacombe, Torquay on the 30th July and to the Royal Hippodrome, Eastbourne on the 2nd September.

Jet met up with Bobby Graham towards the end of the year. Bobby, who was voted the UK's number one session drummer (over 15000 recordings) hit it off with Jet immediately and they got together to record 'Diamonds Are Trumps' early 2001. To promote the new CD Jet was to support Bobby and his band at the

Ponderosa on the island in April 2001 and Huntingdon Hall, Worcester in October of that year.

Vic decided to resurrect the show from 2000 with an improved package including John Leyton, again putting the show on at The Medina in May and the following month at the Ashcroft Theatre Croydon. The same show was to return again at the same venues in March and August the following year 2003. September 2003, found Jet back at the Medina for a one off package with The Bruvvers supporting The Searchers. The word was starting to get around, Vic being approached by a Swedish promoter, Hans Edlar early in 2003 with the view to staging the show sometime later in Holland. Hans had taken an interest after watching them, and booked Jet along with The Rapiers, Johnny and the Hurricanes, The Sputniks and The Tornados, at the London Palladium with Jet topping the bill. Jet recalled that Bruce Welch came along and was most impressed. Bruce hadn't really had any dealings with Jet doing his own thing with his own band.

The meeting with Vic was to be the kick-start that he needed. Vic staging around forty shows for Jet, featuring Mike Berry, John Leyton together with The Rapiers. Vic had his doubts at first as to whether Jet could perform. Jet had a reputation that was second to none and it always went before him. His addiction to the bottle had given numerous agents and promoters serious doubts as to whether he could actually still 'do it' to the standard that the venues required. Vic had contacted Mark Lundquist himself a musician who played guitar for

MIKE COOK

Cliff Bennett and the Rebel Rousers with the view to putting Jet on the road.

Jet found himself once again in the public eye. A visit from the After They Were Famous TV show and David Frost's Through The Keyhole found him back on the small screen. This sense of a 'reprieve' gave him even more determination to continue the road to a full recovery from alcohol.

The meeting with Jet had fired Vic's imagination. He unlike many before him, who had fallen by the wayside, the chance he had taken was seemingly beginning to pay off. The three years had proved to be fairly successful Jet remaining stone sober; His new found belief had gone down well with a lot of people. He had now been 'dry' for nearly three years. Work began to come in albeit slowly at first. The Rapiers who had been with him virtually from the start never lost faith in his ability and soon many shows were to follow. His determination to succeed both musically and mentally spurred him on. The lure of alcohol seemed like a distant nightmare.

2003 was to be tinged with sadness when Winnie passed away, aged 91. As a mother she was everything a mother should be. Jet always maintained that she was a bit of an old bugger, occasionally cantankerous and difficult to live with. She was a remarkable woman who kept herself fit taking up line dancing at 87 years of age! Alec always spoke highly of her and her strength and tenacity kept Jet going for many years during her time in Upton St Leonards. Jet was a very trying person to live with but Winnie never ever gave up on him. Her memory lives on in his garden. Winnie was to remain locked away in a cupboard at the undertakers for three years until 2006 when Jan and Wendy, Mike's wife brought her home to rest.

Jet and Jan had planted a rose in memory of his father Bill. The rose had been planted there some years before and had never flowered. After a small celebration her remains were placed beside the rose and amazingly within three months its leaves began to colour and a rose appeared. Strange or what?....

During the interim years Jet continued to rebuild his life. He had not had a drink since 1999. Suddenly he was a nice person to know. Most of the concerts featured The Rapiers who now had been associated with Jet for nigh on 20 years. Vic had got an idea in mind to feature Jet and set about writing a tribute show 'The Best Of Me' to his friend Sir Cliff Richard late 2003 early 2004. The show would eventually take in 28 venues and after many hours of rehearsals opened at The Epsom Playhouse June 2004 and continued till May 2005.

Vic Farrow had spoken with Jet about the possibility of putting a tribute show together featuring the band along with Cliff Hall who had worked with various members of The Shadows including Sir Cliff himself. He contacted Jimmy Jemain who featured in 'Stars In Their Eyes' impersonating Cliff who jumped at the chance to do the show. He set to work writing the script. Within a matter of weeks rehearsals got under way. The show 'The Best Of Me' hit the road, taking in theatres the length and breadth of the country, under the management and representation of Vic along with All Electric Productions. Cliff Hall began his musical career way back in the sixties, playing with the Oscar Rabin Band and the late Lonnie Donegan. He has also featured on many sessions and recordings with Eric Clapton and the late George Harrison. Having done numerous TV appearances accompanying Sammy Davis Jnr, Michael Jackson and Tony Bennett, Cliff was the ideal man to have in the team.

Jet and Jan hadn't seen Mike and Wendy for over six years. The show was scheduled for Buxton and all four of them met up at the theatre. Mike and Wendy were living in South Yorkshire and had fancied a move back to the sea. Jet insisted on them coming over for a visit and taking up the offer they too were to find themselves living on the island by October 2005.

The show appeared to be going from strength to strength picking up some good reviews. The whole cast was about to lose a valued member and dear friend. Within weeks of appearing at the Middlesbrough Theatre, Wayne Nicholls who played rhythm guitar with the Rapiers together with his wife Jackie tragically lost their lives in a motorbike accident. Jet and Jan along with the band were devastated. Wayne and Jackie were two of the nicest people you could have ever wished to meet. The respect he had gained from fellow musicians shone out with many of them including Bruce Welch and Mike Berry giving their services for free at a charity gig for the children that were so tragically left behind.

Jet celebrated his 65th birthday with a 'Pension Party' in the garden of the cottage. Members of both The Rapiers, The Commotions and The Bruvvers came along. Jet not only found himself entertaining friends on the island but also in Bristol on July 3rd. three days before his official birthday. A gig at Ludlow Castle in Shropshire with the Bruvvers followed on the 10th, returning back home to the island for a couple of shows at Shanklin theatre on the 18th July and the 8th of August. An appearance with John Leyton at Warners Corton Lowestoft rounded off August.

Buxton Opera House and The Forum Theatre at Billingham on the 8th and 9th September were followed by three shows at the Princes Theatre, Hunstanton on the 12th, Theatre Royal, Margate on the 15th, and Farnham Hall, Fareham along with Mike Berry and John Leyton. The Olympiad Leisure Centre, Chippenham rounded off September on the 25th.

Jet had finally turned the corner. He had at last regained his dignity. People were beginning to sit up and take notice. October saw him take in 6 gigs in 16 days. The Swan at Worcester on the 1st, Sevenoaks on the 7th, Perton, Wolverhampton the 8th, The Tivoli Theatre, Wimbourne on the 9th, Fairfield Concert Hall, Croydon on the 14th, culminating with a final gig on the 16th in Holland. November didn't throw much work his way doing only one gig at Warners Cricket St Thomas in Somerset on the 20th. Jet was now well and truly established on the island. They had taken him to their hearts. Vic Farrow put him in at the Medina Theatre Newport for the Christmas show on the 12th December to round off a reasonable year. Jet was proving people wrong all the time getting stronger and stronger. He didn't need a drink. He had begun to take complete control of his life and his own destiny. People wanted to see him, to shake his hand and above to give him the warmth he had lost in those forgotten years. Next year, 2005 - could only get better.

The Bedford Corn Exchange kicked off the year followed by five gigs in February taking in The Music Hall, Shrewsbury, Harrow Arts Centre, Bedworth Civic Hall, The Octagon Theatre, Yeovil and The Garrick Theatre, Lichfield. March took only two gigs, Princes Hall Aldershot, Kings Hall and Winter Gardens Ilkley. Jet found himself travelling up to the Middlesbrough Theatre on April 2nd completing the gigs for the month at Castle Hall, Hertford, on the 9th, Royal Spa Leamington 15th, and The Kings Theatre Southsea on the 16th. It was decided that 'The Best Of Me' although still attracting people, had to be wound down. The expense of staging the show, the length and breadth of the country, being the deciding factor. The hard work had been done. Jet had established himself and the future looked promising. July 2005 found many friends rolling up for Jet's sixty-sixth birthday, celebrating in great style by way of a get together in the garden. Friends from all over the country made their way to the cottage in Peacock Hill.

Another one off show found Jet yet again at the Medina Theatre. 'From The Shadows' along with Rapiers and Cliff Hall. Vic had again promoted the gig and this found Jet in a more laid-back mood, talking more to the audience about his life and times with The Shadows.

Shadowmania hosted by Bruce Welch was again on the horizon, with tribute bands appearing at The Lakeside Frimley Green climaxing with Jet and The Rapiers. The fans had talked to Jet many times about how all four of the original Shadows were all still alive and how nice it would be to see them all perform together for old times sake. Bruce and Hank who regularly tour with Brian Bennett, Tony's replacement way back in the sixties, had toyed with the idea of a reunion but nothing ever came to fruition. This was probably down to Jet's past record even though Bruce knew he was 'teetotal' . This sadly was never going to happen.

Tony Meehan died tragically at the age of 62. Bruce rang Jet with the news. He was devastated. Tony had fallen down a set of stairs banging his head. He never regained consciousness. Cliff and Bruce attended the funeral, along with many other friends from the sixties. Tony left a legacy of not only good drumming but many fine instrumentals as well. 'Tall Texan' being the one featured by Jet in his act.

Jet had still kept in touch with his old 'flame' Billie Davies. Jet and Billie along with Cliff Hall and The Rapiers had put a show together and were getting rave reviews. Gone were the days when the promoters didn't want to take a chance. Jet had turned it completely round. He was now commanding their attention. The work was once again started to roll in. Jet never wanted to succeed as much as he did now. He would spend hours practising the numerous guitar solos and riffs to make it note perfect, something he had hardly ever done in the past due to the influence of the bottle.

It had to be right. Nothing else would do. He was now in charge of his own destiny. Jan too would often appear alongside him on stage adding the extra vocals when needed. Jet never wanted to leave the island, only doing so when required to work on the mainland. With the majority of his work on the mainland, he had no option but to make the endless trips across the Solent sometimes returning some eighteen hours later with just a cup of coffee for company on the ferry.

The Rapiers under the guidance of Colin Pryce-Jones with Nathan Hulse on bass and John Tuck on Drums, were the most reliable source of income for Jet since the sixties. They knew him inside out unlike the earlier days when the occasional note would go 'astray' Jet was now playing better than ever. Releasing two more CD's , 'The Phoenix Rises' (Mustang Music) early 2000 featuring four of the late Jerry Lordan compositions, and 'Diamonds Are Trumps' (Solent Records) featuring Bobby Graham on drums. Bobby was one of the main session men of the sixties, working with The Kinks to Tom Jones.

March 2006 found Jet at the prestigious Stables, Milton Keynes a theatre run by Johnny Dankworth and Cleo Laine on the 2nd March, followed by Northwich Memorial Hall Cheshire on the 3rd and a return to Perton Civic Centre Wolverhampton on the 4th. Butlins, Skegness on the 20th followed by a gig on home territory at Warners on the Isle of Wight, The Bruvvers providing the backing, along with Cliff Hall. Millfield Theatre Edmonton finished off the month on the 31st, with a gig at The Tivoli Theatre Wimbourne a couple of days before taking the show back to the Medina.

The Annual Eddie Cochran Festival at Chippenham on the 16th April found Jet appearing once again at the Olympiad Theatre, with a return gig to Huntingdon Hall Worcester on the 27th. The Medina show in April 2006 proved to be a huge success. Jet had promoted the show. Many old friends turned up see the show including Nigel Hopkins a record producer who ran a studio at the Lighthouse, Portland Bill. Nigel had worked with many great names including Count Basie as a trumpet player. Nigel was impressed by what he saw and invited Jet to come over and record a new CD at his studios. Jet had already had Cliff Hall over to the cottage to write some new riffs possibly for recording and the three of them got down to the serious business of putting the new record together.

From the recording sessions a new tune emerged that took everybody by storm. San Antonio written by Nigel took to the airways being featured on Isle of Wight Radio and BBC Solent with Richard Cartridge. People from all over the island began to sit up and take notice. They wanted a copy and the switchboard at the local station was 'jammed' for forty-five minutes after the show, the reaction was phenomenal. Such was the response that a limited number of signed copies were issued in September. Jet reckoned like many others that this was the best thing he had recorded since 'Diamonds'.

Fareham found Jet appearing alongside John Leyton and his old friend from Solent Radio Richard Cartridge,

Richard doing an impromptu tribute to Cliff. Another visit to Bruce's 'Shadowmania' in September at Frimley finished off the month. Jet and Nigel continue to write, Jet travelling over a couple of times each month to complete the recordings.

Since the move to the island in 2000 Jet had stayed dry, regaining some much needed self-esteem and self worth that had gone 'missing' on so many occasions before. Away from the temptation his life has been turned upside down - a complete reversal. Life for him took on a whole new meaning, being alcohol free gave him freedom to fight another day. The dark overcast cloud that used to follow him had been lifted. Sunshine filled the autumn days of his life.

A meeting with fellow muso and friend Davey Graham of the Tornados followed. Davey along with his wife Nicki had taken up residency on the island a few years before. Davey had suggested to Jet that they should record a DVD, as a teaching aid to playing the guitar, with the view to releasing it on general sale to the public. Jet loved the idea, and couldn't wait to do it. The Bugle Inn in Brading offered the facilities, with Davey and Jet offering advice on simple guitar chords. This recording was to be the final official thing that Jet was to record. Davey said that it was privilege and a pleasure to play alongside Jet, even though because of his reputation, he didn't think he would offer the time.

Jet divided his time between his beloved garden and close friends meeting up whenever they were able for a coffee or a cup of Earl Grey, at The Windmill, Bembridge or The Kings House in Sandown. Looking over Sandown Bay, gave him such a warm feeling inside. He often compared it to his favourite view from the big window in the Fowey Hotel overlooking Fowey estuary. He had good taste. Sir Cliff always stayed there when ever he appeared in Cornwall. Now in the late autumn of his life, his head was awash with so many memories, photos adorning the walls of the tiny cottage, hidden away from the madding crowd. He was smiling once again.

The days of rolling in from The Vauxhall and Molly Malone's in Barton Street, Gloucester were far behind him. He had turned his life completely around from a drunken no-hoper to topping the bill at the London Palladium, unlike his planned gig in Shanklin some year's earlier, turning up a week early at the theatre due to his precarious state of mind induced by alcohol! It was a pleasure not to hear the landlord shout...

'TIME GENTLEMEN PLEASE!'

It all seemed to be going so well but within eighteen months it was to change dramatically. Janet his rock for the last ten years was beginning to fade. Living with anybody has its ups and downs, but living with Jet was another matter. They had begun to tire of each other, so much so that Jet had 'discovered ' another admirer, Janet Hemingway who lived in Winchester. He had talked with Mike at length about her and when the break finally came after a meeting at The Windmill, he decided to go for it. The marriage to Janet Harris was as good as over, she had met someone else albeit in the last two months of their relationship, unlike Jet who had already spent time with 'friends' according to him in Winchester! It was 2007.

One day at Glovers Cottages, Jet took a telephone call. Marty Wilde had offered Jet a spot on his forthcoming tour and with work not too forthcoming he jumped at the opportunity to perform. The new Janet in his life like the previous one had always been a life long fan. the chance to meet and mingle with other sixties legends along with Marty threw her into a different world. Her life like Jet's, was to take an unrehearsed and totally unforeseen move.

Jet had always been a heavy smoker. Tobacco along with the cannabis he grew at the cottage seemed to fill the air twenty four hours a day. His drinking to the outside world had stopped. Secretly he was still taking the odd one here and there. During one of the gigs with Marty, Mike took a call from Jet asking him to come and get him although he didn't know at the time where he was. He had succumbed to a glass or two of wine at one of the gigs. Both Wendy and Mike along with others had warned Janet about this problem and had told her that he mustn't ever drink any alcohol. Jet of course knew different. Mike rang Nigel his recording manager at Portland and it was left up to Billie Davis's close associate Ralph Gowling to pick up the pieces.

During this period Mike's wife Wendy passed away suddenly. Jet couldn't handle it. He had known Wendy for many years. He didn't go to the funeral, although he was only twenty five miles away. He could never handle funerals. Mike had desperately wanted him there. It wasn't to be.

The tour culminated at the London Palladium. He was joined on stage by Hank, Bruce and Brian. This was to be the last time he would ever perform with fellow members of The Shadows. Cliff had talked of doing a farewell world tour with The Shadows and Jet was hoping as an original member to join them. Most people were surprised at his non inclusion, but the risk could not be taken. His reputation had still followed him all these years later, even though he had virtually stopped drinking, the chance could not be taken.. He once told Mike that smoking cannabis kept him off the bottle, but it was just an excuse. He gigged on and off for the next year, sharing his time between Winchester and Peacock Hill. Although nearly seventy he was still pulling people in and never gave a bad show. Jet was still using The Rapiers who had been with him for many years, and probably the best backing group in the country when it came to Shadows music. Under the guidance of Colin Pryce-Jones, Jet was secure in the knowledge that if he missed a note as he often did, the boys in the band would cover the mistake. Jet said that he had never seen Colin drop a note, mind you he said he did drop one of those old ten bob ones once. According to Jet, Colin and his wife Janet had a stash of old money, just in case it ever made a comeback!

Cliff Hall did the honours on keyboards. Cliff had held Jet in great esteem for many years. A gig at Fareham found relations between Cliff and Jet becoming a little strained. Cliff was suddenly being cold shouldered by everyone around him, especially Jet. During the recording of The Journey, produced by Nigel Hopkins, Jet insisted that Cliff be at the studio to help with the writing of the album. Cliff had wanted to spend time with his grandchildren. Jet had other ideas. He demanded that he had to be there. Jet had always been a taker, never a giver. Cliff suddenly wasn't flavour of the month.

Jet wasn't that keen on practice, and especially learning new tunes. From the early days of the sixties when Diamonds reached number one, it was Joe Moretti who played the original also doing the honours on Scarlet O'Hara and Applejack. Jet had to learn them all! Due to Jet's difficulty in learning new tunes, the album tooklonger than expected. 'The Journey' was though worth waiting for, and probably without doubt the best thing he had recorded in years. Along with Nigel and Paul Rumble on lead guitar the album flowed brilliantly. Cliff Hall's decision to spend time with his family really riled Jet. The seed had been sown. It was to be Cliff's last gig with Jet.

Within a matter of months, Billie Davis and The Rapiers were no longer needed. Billie had been arranging gigs, Jet deciding not to appear. His attitude towards fellow muso's and especially Billie had turned everyone against him. The split with The Rapiers would never be repaired. To their credit they always treated Jet with the greatest respect,and on many occasions his reciprocation to them went without saying. He always knew deep down that they were the best. Sadly they parted company.

Jet continued to gig with Mike Berry and John Leyton, using The Flames for the rest of his playing career.

His new partner was still learning about the business. Janet Hemingway did her best to keep Jet on the straight and narrow, shielding him from the general public and sadly from some of his close friends. Within months, Jet's health began to deteriorate very quickly. He had always been a man of small stature, but he was beginning to lose weight. An invitation the palace to receive an M.B.E from the Queen, for services to music lifted his spirits. For good or for bad he had been a part of history, and this recognition said it all. But all was not well.

He had always been a fighter. He was about to embark on his biggest fight ever....for life.

Towards the end of 2009 his health took a serious turn for the worse. He had been diagnosed with throat cancer. During the next eighteen months he endured many sessions of chemotherapy, and at one time he thought they had caught it.

Marty who was so pleased with Jet's performances on his earlier tour, decided to offer him the chance to tour again with another sixties 'old timer' Eden Kane. Jet was always a survivor,and did his best to fulfil the dates. By the end of February 2011 he was too ill to continue. He never once thought that he was going to die, his inner belief in himself and his will to keep performing drove him on, but sadly it was to be of no avail.

Terence 'Jet' Harris, passed away at 1.45am on the 18th March 2011.

Basingstoke Crematorium found friends, family, and fellow musicians all there to pay their respects. The simple bamboo coffin was adorned with the trilby hat he always wore, and the M.B.E., he had received some months before from the Queen. At the end of the ceremony, as a mark of respect, his life long friend and one time girlfriend Billie Davis, released two white doves to send him on his way.

He had been up so many mornings searching for that light at the end of the tunnel. The days of wandering aimlessly home in the cold night air feeling the bite of the beer within his belly were gone. Living with Jet Harris had been hard work. It was as if God willed he would have to learn many more lessons. Time is a very precious thing. If there were more lessons to be learned then Jet will not allow himself the displeasure of failing and falling back like on so many occasions before.

Nothing in his life came easy. Some people might say that his life has been too easy. There were days when he found it hard to smile. He above all people knew that you can only earn love and respect. That must come from within, a self-belief, an inner knowledge that can only be gained on the journey through life. His love of the simple life can be found summed up in a nutshell on the stone beside his cottage. 'Mainland not far enough'

The island gave him that inner peace...

'They used to open at eleven o'clock'......

DISCOGRAPHY

JET HARRIS AND TONY MEEHAN

The Singles

Diamonds/Footstomp Decca F11563 January 1963.

Scarlet O'Hara/Hully Gully Decca F11644 April 1963.

Applejack/ Tall Texan Decca F11710 August 1963

Diamonds/Scarlet O'Hara Decca 12877   1969.

Diamonds/Scarlet O'Hara Decca 1976

Diamonds/Scarlet O'Hara London Records OG9332 Nov 83.

The EP's

Scarlet O'Hara /Hully Gully/Diamonds/Footstomp Decca DFE8528 June 1963

Diamonds/Scarlet O'Hara/Applejack/ The Man With The Golden Arm (Main Title Theme) Decca F13892 1980.

The LP's

JET HARRIS & TONY MEEHAN Decca LPD289-Y Mono

JET HARRIS & TONY MEEHAN REMEMBERING Decca REM1 Mono.

JET HARRIS & TONY MEEHAN VOL2 Decca LPD297-Y Mono

JET HARRIS & TONY MEEHAN DIAMONDS Decca TAB68 Mono

JET HARRIS & TONY MEEHAN DIAMONDS AND OTHER GEMS Deram Records 820634-2 Mono

JET HARRIS The singles with Cliff Richard and The   Drifters The 78's

High Class Baby/My Feet Hit The Ground 45-DB4203 Nov 1958

Livin' Lovin' Doll/Steady With you 45-DB4249 Jan 1959

Mean Streak/Never Mind 45-DB4306 April 1959

Living Doll/Apron Strings 45-DB4306 July 1959.

CLIFF RICHARD and THE SHADOWS The 78's

Travellin' Light/Dynamite 45-DB4341 Oct. 1959

A Voice In The Wilderness/Don't Be Mad At Me 45-DB4398 Jan 1960.

All the above have also been recorded on 45's

The 45's

Don't Be Mad At Me /Little Things Mean A Lot February 1960.

A Voice In The Wilderness / Love March 1960.

Fall In Love With You /Willie And The Hand Jive 45-DB4431 March 1960

Fall In Love With You/Mean Women Blues April 1960

Please Don't Tease /Where Is My Heart 45-DB4479 June 1960.

Ready Teddy/ Bongo Blues (The Shadows) August 1960.

Nine Times Out Of Ten /Thinking Of Our Love 45-DB4506 Sept 1960.

I Love you / 'D' In Love 45-Db4547 November 1960.

Theme For A Dream /Mumblin' Mosie 45-DB4593 February 1961.

Gee Whiz Its you /I Cannot Find a True Love 45-DC756 March 1961.

A Girl Like You /Now's The Time To Fall In Love 45-DB4667 June 1961.

When The Girl In Your Arms/Got A Funny Feeling 45-DB4716 Oct.1961.

Forty Days / Y'arriva' 1961.

The Young Ones/ We Say Yeah 45-DB 4761 January 1962.

I'll See You In My Dreams/ Dream April 1962.

Lessons In Love/ First Lesson In Love 1962.

The Drifters The 78's

Feelin' Fine/ Don't Be A Fool With Love DB4263 February 1959.

Driftin'/ Jet Black DB4325 June 1959.

THE SHADOWS

The 78's

Saturday Dance/Lonesome Fella DB4387 December 1959.
(also released as a 45)

The 45's

Apache/quartermasters Stores 45-DB4484 July 1960.

The Stranger/ Man Of Mystery 45-DB 4530 Nov 1960.

FBI / Midnight 45-DB4580 February 1961.

The Frightened City/ Back Home 45-DB4637 April 1961.

Kon-Tiki / 36-24-36 45-DB4968 September 1961.

The Savage / Peace Pipe 45-DB4726 November 1961.

Wonderful Land /stars Fell On Stockton 45-Db4970 February 1962.

The EP's

THE SHADOWS Columbia SEG8061 Mono ESG 7834 Stereo Jan. 1961

Mustang/ Theme From Shane/ Shotgun/ Theme From Giant.

THE SHADOWS TO THE FORE Columbia SEG 8094 Mono June 1961.

Apache/ Man Of Mystery/ The Stranger/ FBI

SPOTLIGHT ON THE SHADOWS Columbia SEG 8135 Mono Feb. 1962

OUT OF THE SHADOWS Germany. emidisc 1C 048-50 726 Stereo 1971.

Jet Harris

Other featured Album recordings.

THE SHADOWS GREATEST HITS. Columbia 33SX1522 Mono

1522 Stereo. June 1963.

THE SHADOWS BEST SELLERS. Germany Columbia C83 519 Mono 1963.

THE GREAT SHADOWS Germany Columbia C83 519 Mono 1963.

BRILLIANT SHADOWS BRILLIANT SONGS Germany Columbia C83

609 Mono 1963.

SOMETHIN' ELSE! THE SHADOWS Regal Starline SRS5012 Stereo

Nov 1969.

STARS,HITS,EVERFGREEN, THE SHADOWS. Germany Crystal 028

CRY04 203 Stereo December 1977.

THE SHADOWS VOL 3 British hits Revival. Germany emidisc 1C 048-51

765 Stereo 1972.

THE SHADOWS MFP Label 1388 Stereo July 1970.

(The above album was also released in England August 1970, Germany 1970,and also by Ember –Explosion SE8031 Stereo in 1975)

THE BEST OF THE SHADOWS Germany Columbia 1C 148-04 859/860 Stereo 1972.

MUSTANG- THE SHADOWS MFP Label MFP5266 Stereo Oct. 1972.

THE SHADOWS TWENTY GOLDEN GREATS EMI EMTV3 Stereo

February 1977. (also released in Germany)

THE SHADOWS AT THE MOVIES. MFP Label MFP50 347 Stereo

January 1978.

THE BEST OF THE SHADOWS Germany. EMI 66382 Stereo May 1978.

ROCK WITH THE SHADOWS MFP Label MFP 50 468 Stereo 1980.

THE WORLD RECORD CLUB has also issed a boxed edition which

Features Jet Harris. WORLD RECORD CLUB SM 721-726 Stereo.

JET WAS TO FEATURE ON NUMEROUS LP'S AND CD'S **WITH TANGENT, THE DIAMONDS, CLIFF HALL, THE RAPIERS and THE STRANGERS**

THE CD'S (since 1980's)

THE TWO OF US featuring ALAN JONES 1988

BEYOND A SHADOW OF A DOUBT with TANGENT 1993

JET HARRIS & TANGENT WARM TURN 1994

FISTFUL OF STRINGS 1999

THE PHOENIX RISES 1999

DIAMONDS ARE TRUMPS FEATURING BOBBY GRAHAM 2002

SAN ANTONIO (limited edition single) 2007

THE JOURNEY 2007

Lightning Source UK Ltd.
Milton Keynes UK
UKOW01f0718011116
286592UK00001B/14/P